HBR'S 10 MUST READS

The definitive
management ideas
of the year from
Harvard Business Review.

2018

HBR's 10 Must Reads series is the definitive collection of ideas and best practices for aspiring and experienced leaders alike. These books offer essential reading selected from the pages of *Harvard Business Review* on topics critical to the success of every manager.

Titles include:

HBR's 10 Must Reads 2015
HBR's 10 Must Reads 2016
HBR's 10 Must Reads 2017
HBR's 10 Must Reads 2018
HBR's 10 Must Reads for New Managers
HBR's 10 Must Reads on Change Management
HBR's 10 Must Reads on Collaboration
HBR's 10 Must Reads on Communication
HBR's 10 Must Reads on Emotional Intelligence
HBR's 10 Must Reads on Innovation
HBR's 10 Must Reads on Leadership
HBR's 10 Must Reads on Making Smart Decisions
HBR's 10 Must Reads on Managing Across Cultures
HBR's 10 Must Reads on Managing People
HBR's 10 Must Reads on Managing Yourself
HBR's 10 Must Reads on Sales
HBR's 10 Must Reads on Strategic Marketing
HBR's 10 Must Reads on Strategy
HBR's 10 Must Reads on Teams
HBR's 10 Must Reads: The Essentials

HBR'S
10
MUST
READS

The definitive
management ideas
of the year from
Harvard Business Review.

2018

HARVARD BUSINESS REVIEW PRESS
Boston, Massachusetts

Copyright 2018 Harvard Business School Publishing Corporation
All rights reserved
Printed in the United States of America
10 9 8 7 6 5 4 3 2 1

No part of this publication may be reproduced, stored in or introduced into a retrieval system, or transmitted, in any form, or by any means (electronic, mechanical, photocopying, recording, or otherwise), without the prior permission of the publisher. Requests for permission should be directed to permissions@hbsp.harvard.edu, or mailed to Permissions, Harvard Business School Publishing, 60 Harvard Way, Boston, Massachusetts 02163.

The web addresses referenced in this book were live and correct at the time of the book's publication but may be subject to change.

Cataloging-in-Publication data is forthcoming.

ISBN: 9781633693067
eISBN: 9781633693074

The paper used in this publication meets the requirements of the American National Standard for Permanence of Paper for Publications and Documents in Libraries and Archives Z39.48-1992.

Contents

Editors' Note

Every year, as we build each issue of *Harvard Business Review*, we examine the most important challenges facing business leaders today, from technology to people management. Rather than simply monitoring buzzwords or headlines, this involves a combination of looking forward to how businesses will need to incorporate new technologies and contextual realities, and also looking back at lingering management problems to find the ways that researchers and practitioners are addressing them today. The standout articles of the year collected here, for example, explain emerging phenomena like blockchain, dataviz literacy, and algorithms in practical terms. They also offer new perspectives on long-term issues such as boosting employee engagement, increasing diversity, and fixing the U.S. health care system. We showcase these and other critical themes highlighted by our authors from the past year of *Harvard Business Review* in this volume.

In today's crowded and competitive marketplace, companies often feel pressure to rebrand or expand their offerings to stay alive. But P&G's A.G. Lafley and strategy expert and Rotman School of Management professor Roger L. Martin say companies should focus their efforts on strengthening customers' habits, not developing products or redesigning packaging. In **"Customer Loyalty Is Overrated,"** the authors acknowledge that although it's hard work to establish a brand, once you've done so, constant reinvention won't keep customers coming back. Research suggests that what makes competitive advantage sustainable is helping consumers avoid expending the mental energy to make a choice. Customers don't want to have to evaluate their options every time they shop; they just want to buy what they've always bought. And each time customers pick the same product, they boost its advantage over that of the products they didn't choose.

Inconsistent decision making is often a hidden and expensive problem plaguing companies—not the big, sweeping, strategy-related choices, but the daily decisions and judgment calls, which can swing radically from one individual to the next. This problem affects not just new employees but seasoned people who have been in the same roles, following the same well-established guidelines.

Irrelevant factors, such as mood and the weather, can affect a person's decisions from one occasion to the next. This chance variability of decisions is called *noise*. In **"Noise: How to Overcome the High, Hidden Cost of Inconsistent Decision Making,"** Nobel laureate and Princeton psychology professor Daniel Kahneman and data analysis experts Andrew M. Rosenfield, Linnea Gandhi, and Tom Blaser explain how organizations can perform a "noise audit" and use algorithms and simple commonsense rules to guide employees toward making more-consistent decisions.

Managers should all be relying more on data in their decision making, but it arrives at such velocity, and in such volume, that many of them don't know quite what to do with it. A good first step is to create a visualization or a chart. To do that well, however, you need to understand the nature of your data and keep your purpose in mind, according to Scott Berinato, an HBR senior editor and the author of *Good Charts: The HBR Guide to Making Smarter, More Persuasive Data Visualizations*. That strategic attitude will make your charts and presentations much clearer and more effective. In **"Visualizations That Really Work,"** Berinato outlines categories of approach and the tools and resources you'll need for each.

Managers are pretty good at assessing *whether* a new technology will overtake an existing one, but they haven't quite figured out how to know *when* that will happen. In **"Right Tech, Wrong Time,"** professors Ron Adner and Rahul Kapoor say that not just your new technology but also the ecosystem in which it will exist—the related technologies, services, standards, and regulations—can influence how quickly it's adopted. They provide a framework to assess how soon disruptive change is coming to your industry by analyzing the dynamics of the context in which it will exist. If the new technology doesn't need a new ecosystem to support it—if it's essentially plug-and-play—adoption will be swift. But if complements are needed (for example, electric cars require a network of charging stations), the pace of substitution will slow until those challenges have been resolved.

How to pay for health care is a problem the United States has struggled with for a long time. Fee-for-service, the dominant model today, is widely recognized as the single biggest obstacle to improving health care delivery, because it rewards the quantity rather than the quality or efficiency of care. What we need is a system that rewards providers for delivering superior value to patients—for achieving better health outcomes at a lower cost. In **"How to Pay for Health Care,"** strategy giants Michael E. Porter and Robert S. Kaplan argue that a "bundled payments" model is the right one, because it triggers competition among providers to create value where it matters—at the individual patient level. They describe robust proof-of-concept initiatives in the United States and abroad that show how the challenges of transitioning to bundled payments are already being overcome.

Another system that's overdue for reform is annual performance reviews. Emphasizing individual accountability for past results, traditional appraisals give short shrift to improving current performance and developing talent for the future. That can hinder long-term competitiveness, say Peter Cappelli and Anna Tavis in **"The Performance Management Revolution."** To better support employee development, many organizations are dropping or radically changing their annual-review systems in favor of giving people less-formal, more-frequent feedback that follows the natural cycle of work. The authors explain how performance management has evolved over the decades and why current thinking has shifted.

Goal-setting and evaluation are one way to motivate your employees, but how to engage them is another long-standing issue for managers and organizations. Francesca Gino, a professor of business administration at Harvard Business School, conducted groundbreaking research and found that whether consciously or unconsciously, organizations pressure employees—including leaders—to reserve their real, authentic, nonconforming selves for outside the workplace. This pressure to conform, she writes in **"Let Your Workers Rebel,"** can have a significant negative impact on engagement, productivity, and the ability to innovate. To fix this problem, she says, develop a culture that supports "constructive nonconformity": encourage your workers to break rules and be themselves.

Diversity programs are another relic in organizations: Most companies rely on the same approach they've been using since the 1960s to reduce bias and increase diversity—one that focuses on controlling managers' behaviors. But as studies have shown, that tends to activate bias rather than quash it, because people rebel against rules that threaten their autonomy. In the McKinsey Award–winning **"Why Diversity Programs Fail,"** Frank Dobbin and Alexandra Kalev draw on their research to suggest ways of promoting diversity that engage employees in working explicitly toward that goal, increase contact with female and minority colleagues to lessen bias, and encourage social accountability through transparency and diversity task forces.

The U.S. presidential election in November 2016 left in its wake a question that also resonates in other countries experiencing populist upwellings: How did the liberal political establishment, media, and electorate fail to anticipate the anger and desperate desire for change that ushered in the Trump administration? In **"What So Many People Don't Get About the U.S. Working Class,"** Joan C. Williams, a distinguished professor of law at UC Hastings, points her finger at "class cluelessness" and draws on her expertise in labor and social class to describe to "professional elites" the difference between "working-class" and poor, the role of the urban-rural divide, the need for job and college programs, and how race and gender do (and don't!) play a part in working-class politics.

We've all heard that blockchain will revolutionize business. But what is it? And when will organizations need to integrate it into their daily operations? In **"The Truth About Blockchain,"** Marco Iansiti and Karim R. Lakhani, academics who study digital innovation in business, explain this new technology and assure us that its arrival is going to take a lot longer than many people claim. Like TCP/IP (on which the internet was built), blockchain is a foundational technology that will require broad coordination. Its level of complexity— technological, regulatory, and social—will be unprecedented. It could transform the economy by slashing the cost of transactions (and how long they take) and eliminating intermediaries such as lawyers and bankers. The adoption of TCP/IP suggests that blockchain will follow a fairly predictable path. But although the journey may take years, it's not too early to start planning.

New technology is born of effective R&D, but numerous potential stumbling blocks lie between research and commercial development. Early-stage research is expensive, risky, and unpredictable—so corporations generally shy away from it, leaving many opportunities unexplored. They could revitalize their research operations by adopting the approach taken by Bob Langer, a chemical engineer whose lab at MIT is one of the most productive and profitable research facilities in the world. **"The Edison of Medicine,"** by HBR senior editor Steven Prokesch, details Langer Lab's proven formula for accelerating the pace of discoveries and getting them into the world as products. It includes focusing on projects that could make the most difference to society, finding opportunity in the constant turnover of researchers, and cultivating a leadership style that balances freedom and support.

Looking across disciplines and trends and synthesizing the best ideas is important—and time-consuming—work for today's leaders. With this volume, we've done some of that heavy lifting for you. With topics ranging from a new type of literacy to a new way to record transactions, the articles here will help you better manage your work today and make smart plans for whatever lies ahead.

—The Editors

Customer Loyalty Is Overrated

by A.G. Lafley and Roger L. Martin

LATE IN THE SPRING OF 2016 Facebook's category-leading photo-sharing application, Instagram, abandoned its original icon, a retro camera familiar to the app's 400-million-plus users, and replaced it with a flat modernist design that, as the head of design explained, "suggests a camera." At a time when Instagram was under a growing threat from its rival Snapchat, he offered this rationale for the switch: The icon "was beginning to feel . . . not reflective of the community, and we thought we could make it better."

The assessment of *AdWeek,* the marketing industry bible, was clear from its headline: "Instagram's New Logo Is a Travesty. Can We Change it Back? Please?" In *GQ*'s article "Logo Change No One Wanted Just Came to Instagram," the magazine's panel of designers called the new icon "honestly horrible," "so ugly," and "trash," and summarized the change thus: "Instagram spent YEARS building up visual brand equity with its existing logo, training users where to tap, and now instead of iterating on that, it's flushing it all down the toilet for the homescreen equivalent of a Starburst."

It's too soon to tell whether the design change will actually have commercial consequences for Instagram, but this is not the first time a company has experienced such a reaction to a rebranding or a relaunch. PepsiCo's introduction of its aspartame-free Diet Pepsi was—like the infamous New Coke debacle—a botched attempt at reinvention that resulted in serious revenue losses and had to be reversed. The interesting question, therefore, is: Why do well-performing companies routinely succumb to the lure of radical rebranding? One could understand the temptation to adopt such a strategy in the face of disaster, but Instagram, PepsiCo, and Coke were hardly staring into the abyss. (It's worth noting that Snapchat, whose market share among young users is now particularly strong, has assiduously stuck to its familiar ghost icon. Full disclosure: A.G. Lafley serves on the board of Snap Inc.)

The answer, we believe, is rooted in some serious misperceptions about the nature of competitive advantage. Much new thinking in strategy argues that the fast pace of change in modern business (perhaps nowhere more obvious than in the app world) means no competitive advantage is sustainable, so companies must continually update their business models, strategies, and communications to respond in real time to the explosion of choice that ever more sophisticated consumers now face. To keep your customers—and to attract new ones—you need to remain relevant and superior. Hence Instagram was doing exactly what it was supposed to do: changing proactively.

That's an edgy thought, to be sure; but a lot of evidence contradicts it. Consider Southwest Airlines, Vanguard, and IKEA, all featured in Michael Porter's classic 1996 HBR article "What Is Strategy?" as exemplars of long-lived competitive advantage. A full two decades later those companies are still at the top of their respective industries, pursuing largely unchanged strategies and branding. And although Google, Facebook, or Amazon might stumble and be crushed by some upstart, the competitive positions of those giants hardly look fleeting. Closer to home (one author of this article is part of the P&G family), it would strike the Tide or Head & Shoulders brand managers of the past 50 years as rather odd to hear that their half-century advantages have not been or are not sustainable. (No doubt the Unilever managers of long-standing consumer favorites such as Dove soap and Hellmann's mayonnaise would feel the same.)

In this article we draw on modern behavioral research to offer a theory about what makes competitive advantage last. It explains

Idea in Brief

The Problem

Product innovations often flame out on launch, despite tremendous efforts to make them attractive, relevant, and up-to-date.

Why It Happens

Customers don't want to spend the mental energy needed to choose between products.

The Solution

To strengthen customers' habits, innovations should represent a progression of the brand rather than a break with the past.

both missteps like Instagram's and success stories like Tide's. We argue that performance is sustained not by offering customers the perfect choice but by offering them the easy one. So even if a value proposition is what first attracted them, it is not necessarily what keeps them coming.

In this alternative worldview, holding on to customers is not a matter of continually adapting to changing needs in order to remain the rational or emotional best fit. It's about helping customers avoid having to make yet another choice. To do that, you have to create what we call *cumulative advantage*.

Let's begin by exploring what our brains actually do when we shop.

Creatures of Habit

The conventional wisdom about competitive advantage is that successful companies pick a position, target a set of consumers, and configure activities to serve them better. The goal is to make customers repeat their purchases by matching the value proposition to their needs. By fending off competitors through ever-evolving uniqueness and personalization, the company can achieve sustainable competitive advantage.

An assumption implicit in that definition is that consumers are making deliberate, perhaps even rational, decisions. Their reasons for buying products and services may be emotional, but they always result from somewhat conscious logic. Therefore a good strategy figures out and responds to that logic.

But the idea that purchase decisions arise from conscious choice flies in the face of much research in behavioral psychology. The brain, it turns out, is not so much an analytical machine as a gap-filling machine: It takes noisy, incomplete information from the world and quickly fills in the missing pieces on the basis of past experience. Intuition—thoughts, opinions, and preferences that come to mind quickly and without reflection but are strong enough to act on—is the product of this process. It's not just what gets filled in that determines our intuitive judgments, however. They are heavily influenced by the speed and ease of the filling-in process itself, a phenomenon psychologists call *processing fluency*. When we describe making a decision because it "just feels right," the processing leading to the decision has been fluent.

Processing fluency is itself the product of repeated experience, and it increases relentlessly with the number of times we have the experience. Prior exposure to an object improves the ability to perceive and identify that object. As an object is presented repeatedly, the neurons that code features not essential for recognizing the object dampen their responses, and the neural network becomes more selective and efficient at object identification. In other words, repeated stimuli have lower perceptual-identification thresholds, require less attention to be noticed, and are faster and more accurately named or read. What's more, consumers tend to prefer them to new stimuli.

In short, research into the workings of the human brain suggests that the mind loves automaticity more than just about anything else—certainly more than engaging in conscious consideration. Given a choice, it would like to do the same things over and over again. If the mind develops a view over time that Tide gets clothes cleaner, and Tide is available and accessible on the store shelf or the web page, the easy, familiar thing to do is to buy Tide yet another time.

A driving reason to choose the leading product in the market, therefore, is simply that it is the easiest thing to do: In whatever distribution channel you shop, it will be the most prominent offering. In the supermarket, the mass merchandiser, or the drugstore, it will dominate the shelf. In addition, you have probably bought it before from that very shelf. Doing so again is the easiest possible action you can take. Not only that, but every time you buy another unit of the brand in question, you make it easier to do—for which the mind applauds you.

Meanwhile, it becomes ever so slightly harder to buy the products you didn't choose, and that gap widens with every purchase—as long, of course, as the chosen product consistently fulfills your expectations. This logic holds as much in the new economy as in the old. If you make Facebook your home page, every aspect of that page will be totally familiar to you, and the impact will be as powerful as facing a wall of Tide in a store—or more so.

Buying the biggest, easiest brand creates a cycle in which share leadership is continually increased over time. Each time you select and use a given product or service, its advantage over the products or services you didn't choose cumulates.

The growth of cumulative advantage—absent changes that force conscious reappraisal—is nearly inexorable. Thirty years ago Tide enjoyed a small lead of 33% to 28% over Unilever's Surf in the lucrative U.S. laundry detergent market. Consumers at the time slowly but surely formed habits that put Tide further ahead of Surf. Every year, the habit differential increased and the share gap widened. In 2008 Unilever exited the business and sold its brands to what was then a private-label detergent manufacturer. Now Tide enjoys a greater than 40% market share, making it the runaway leader in the U.S. detergent market. Its largest branded competitor has a share of less than 10%. (For a discussion of why small brands even survive in this environment, see the sidebar "The Perverse Upside of Customer Disloyalty.")

A Complement to Choice

We don't claim that consumer choice is never conscious, or that the quality of a value proposition is irrelevant. To the contrary: People must have a reason to buy a product in the first place. And sometimes a new

The Perverse Upside of Customer Disloyalty

IF CONSUMERS ARE SLAVES OF HABIT, it's hard to argue that they are "loyal" customers in the sense that they consciously attach themselves to a brand on the assumption that it meets rational or emotional needs. In fact, customers are much more fickle than many marketers assume: Often the brands that are believed to depend on loyal customers achieve the lowest loyalty scores.

For example, Colgate and Crest are the leading toothpaste brands in the U.S. market, with about 75% of it between them. Customers for both are loyal 50% of the time (their preferred brand accounts for 50% of their annual toothpaste purchases). Tom's toothpaste, a niche "natural" brand based in Maine, has a 1% market share and is thought to have a fanatical customer following. One might expect the data to show that the 1% are mostly repeat buyers. But in fact Tom's customers are loyal only 25% of the time—half the rate of the big brands.

So why do fringe brands like Tom's survive? The answer, perhaps perversely, is that with big-brand loyalty rates at 50%, just enough customers will buy small brands from time to time to keep the latter in business. But the small brands can't overcome the familiarity barrier, and although entirely new brands do enter categories and become leaders, it is extremely rare for a small fringe brand to successfully take on an established leader.

---

technology or a new regulation enables a company to radically lower a product's price or to offer new features or a wholly new solution to a customer need in a way that demands consumers' consideration.

Robust where-to-play and how-to-win choices, therefore, are still essential to strategy. Without a value proposition superior to those of other companies that are attempting to appeal to the same customers, a company has nothing to build on.

But if it is to extend that initial competitive advantage, the company must invest in turning its proposition into a habit rather than a choice. Hence we can formally define cumulative advantage as the layer that a company builds on its initial competitive advantage by making its product or service an ever more instinctively comfortable choice for the customer.

Companies that don't build cumulative advantage are likely to be overtaken by competitors that succeed in doing so. A good example is Myspace, whose failure is often cited as proof that competitive advantage is inherently unsustainable. Our interpretation is somewhat different.

Launched in August 2003, Myspace became America's number one social networking site within two years and in 2006 overtook Google to become the most visited site of any kind in the United States. Nevertheless, a mere two years later it was outstripped by Facebook, which demolished it competitively—to the extent that Myspace was sold in 2011 for $35 million, a fraction of the $580 million that News Corp had paid for it in 2005.

Why did Myspace fail? Our answer is that it didn't even try to achieve cumulative advantage. To begin with, it allowed users to create web pages that expressed their own personal style, so individual pages looked very different to visitors. It also placed advertising in jarring ways—and included ads for indecent services, which riled regulators. When News Corp bought Myspace, it ramped up ad density, further cluttering the site. To entice more users, Myspace rolled out what *Bloomberg Businessweek* referred to as "a dizzying number of features: communication tools such as instant messaging, a classifieds program, a video player, a music player, a virtual karaoke machine, a self-serve advertising platform, profile-editing tools, security systems, privacy filters, Myspace book lists, and on and on." So instead of making its site an ever more comfortable and instinctive choice, Myspace kept its users off balance, wondering (if not subconsciously worrying) what was coming next.

Compare that with Facebook. From day one, Facebook has been building cumulative advantage. Initially it had some attractive features that Myspace lacked, making it a good value proposition, but more important to its success has been the consistency of its look and feel. Users conform to its rigid standards, and Facebook conforms to nothing or no one else. When it made its now-famous extension from desktop to mobile, the company ensured that users' mobile experience was highly consistent with their desktop experience.

To be sure, Facebook has from time to time introduced design changes in order to better leverage its functionality, and it has endured severe criticism in consequence. But in the main, new service introductions don't jeopardize comfort and familiarity, and the company has often made the changes optional in their initial stages. Even its name conjures up a familiar artifact, the college facebook, whereas Myspace gives the user no familiar reference at all.

Bottom line: By building on familiarity, Facebook has used cumulative advantage to become the most addictive social networking site in the world. That makes its subsidiary Instagram's decision to change its icon all the more baffling.

The Cumulative Advantage Imperatives

Myspace and Facebook nicely illustrate the twin realities that sustainable advantage is both possible and not assured. How, then, might the next Myspace enhance and extend its competitive edge by building a protective layer of cumulative advantage? Here are four basic rules to follow:

1. Become popular early

This idea is far from new—it is implicit in many of the best and earliest works on strategy, and we can see it in the thinking of Bruce Henderson, the founder of Boston Consulting Group. Henderson's particular focus was on the beneficial impact of cumulative output on costs—the now-famous experience curve, which suggests that as a company's experience in making something increases, its cost management becomes more efficient. He argued that companies should price aggressively early on—"ahead of the experience curve," in his parlance—and thus win sufficient market share to give the company lower costs, higher relative share, and higher profitability. The implication was clear: Early share advantage matters—a lot.

Marketers have long understood the importance of winning early. Launched specifically to serve the fast-growing automatic washing machine market, Tide is one of P&G's most revered, successful, and profitable brands. When it was introduced, in 1946, it immediately had the heaviest advertising weight in the category. P&G also made sure that no washing machine was sold in America without a free box of Tide to get consumers' habits started. Tide quickly won the early popularity contest and has never looked back.

Free new-product samples to gain trial have always been a popular tactic with marketers. Aggressive pricing, the tactic favored by Henderson, is similarly popular. Samsung has emerged as the market share leader in the smartphone industry worldwide by providing very affordable Android-based phones that carriers can offer free with service contracts. For internet businesses, free is the core tactic for establishing habits. Virtually all the large-scale internet success stories—eBay, Google, Twitter, Instagram, Uber, Airbnb—make their services free so that users will grow and deepen their habits; then providers or advertisers will be willing to pay for access to them.

2. Design for habit

As we've seen, the best outcome is when choosing your offering becomes an automatic consumer response. So design for that—don't leave the outcome entirely to chance. We've seen how Facebook profits from its attention to consistent, habit-forming design, which has made use of its platform go beyond what we think of as habit: Checking for updates has become a real compulsion for a billion people. Of course Facebook benefits from increasingly huge network effects. But the real advantage is that to switch from Facebook also entails breaking a powerful addiction.

The smartphone pioneer BlackBerry is perhaps the best example of a company that consciously designed for addiction. Its founder, Mike Lazaridis, explicitly created the device to make the cycle of feeling a buzz in the holster, slipping out the BlackBerry, checking the message, and thumbing a response on the miniature keyboard as addictive as possible. He succeeded: The device earned the nickname CrackBerry. The habit was so strong that even after BlackBerry had been brought down by the move to app-based and touch-screen smartphones, a core group of BlackBerry customers—who had staunchly refused to adapt—successfully implored the company's management to bring back a BlackBerry that resembled their previous-generation devices. It was given the comforting name Classic.

As Art Markman, a psychologist at the University of Texas, has pointed out to us, certain rules should be respected in designing for habit. To begin with, you must keep consistent those elements of the product design that can be seen from a distance so that buyers can find your product quickly. Distinctive colors and shapes like Tide's bright orange and the Doritos logo accomplish this.

And you should find ways to make products fit in people's environments to encourage use. When P&G introduced Febreze, consumers liked the way it worked but did not use it often. Part of the problem, it turned out, was that the container was shaped like a glass-cleaner bottle, signaling that it should be kept under the sink. The bottle was ultimately redesigned to be kept on a counter or in a more visible cabinet, and use after purchase increased.

Unfortunately, the design changes that companies make all too often end up disrupting habits rather than strengthening them. Look for changes that will reinforce habits and encourage repurchase. The Amazon Dash Button provides an excellent example: By creating a simple way for people to reorder products they use often, Amazon helps them develop habits and locks them into a particular distribution channel.

3. Innovate inside the brand

As we've already noted, companies engage in initiatives to "relaunch," "repackage," or "replatform" at some peril: Such efforts can require customers to break their habits. Of course companies have to keep their products up-to-date, but changes in technology or other features should ideally be introduced in a manner that allows the new version of a product or service to retain the cumulative advantage of the old.

Even the most successful builders of cumulative advantage sometimes forget this rule. P&G, for example, which has increased Tide's cumulative advantage over 70 years through huge changes, has had to learn some painful lessons along the way. Arguably the first great detergent innovation after Tide's launch was the development of liquid detergents. P&G's first response was to launch a new brand, called Era, in 1975. With no cumulative advantage behind it,

Era failed to become a major brand despite consumers' increasing substitution of liquid for powdered detergent.

Recognizing that as the number one brand in the category, Tide had a strong connection with consumers and a powerful cumulative advantage, P&G decided to launch Liquid Tide in 1984, in familiar packaging and with consistent branding. It went on to become the dominant liquid detergent despite its late entry. After that experience, P&G was careful to ensure that further innovations were consistent with the Tide brand. When its scientists figured out how to incorporate bleach into detergent, the product was called Tide Plus Bleach. The breakthrough cold-cleaning technology appeared in Tide Coldwater, and the revolutionary three-in-one pod form was launched as Tide Pods. The branding could not have been simpler or clearer: This is your beloved Tide, with bleach added, for cold water, in pod form. These comfort- and familiarity-laden innovations reinforced rather than diminished the brand's cumulative advantage. The new products all preserved the look of Tide's traditional packaging—the brilliant orange and the bull's-eye logo. The few times in Tide history when that look was altered—such as with blue packaging for the Tide Coldwater launch—the effect on consumers was significantly negative, and the change was quickly reversed.

Of course, sometimes change is absolutely necessary to maintain relevance and advantage. In such situations smart companies succeed by helping customers transition from the old habit to the new one. Netflix began as a service that delivered DVDs to customers by mail. It would be out of business today if it had attempted to maximize continuity by refusing to change. Instead, it has successfully transformed itself into a video streaming service.

Although the new Netflix markets a completely different platform for digital entertainment, involving a new set of activities, Netflix found ways to help its customers by accentuating what did not have to change. It has the same look and feel and is still a subscription service that gives people access to the latest entertainment without leaving their homes. Thus its customers can deal with the necessary aspects of change while maintaining as much of the habit as possible. For customers, "improved" is much more comfortable and less scary than "new," however awesome "new" sounds to brand managers and advertising agencies.

4. Keep communication simple

One of the fathers of behavioral science, Daniel Kahneman, characterized subconscious, habit-driven decision making as "thinking fast" and conscious decision making as "thinking slow." Marketers and advertisers often seem to live in thinking-slow mode. They are rewarded with industry kudos for the cleverness with which they weave together and highlight the multiple benefits of a new product or service. True, ads that are clever and memorable sometimes move customers to change their habits. The slow-thinking conscious mind, if it decides to pay attention, may well say, "Wow, that is impressive. I can't wait!"

But if viewers aren't paying attention (as in the vast majority of cases), an artful communication may backfire. Consider the ad that came out a couple of years ago for the Samsung Galaxy S5. It began by showing successive vignettes of generic-looking smartphones failing to (a) demonstrate water resistance; (b) protect against a young child's accidentally sending an embarrassing message; and (c) enable an easy change of battery. It then triumphantly pointed out that the Samsung S5, which looked pretty much like the three previous phones, overcame all these flaws. Conscious, slow-thinking viewers, if they watched the whole ad, may have been persuaded that the S5 was different from and superior to other phones. But an arguably greater likelihood was that fast-thinking viewers would subconsciously associate the S5 with the three shortcomings. When making a purchase decision, they might be swayed by a subconscious plea: "Don't buy the one with the water-resistance, rogue-message, and battery-change problems." In fact, the ad might even induce them to buy a competitor's product—such as the iPhone 7—whose message about water resistance is simpler to take in.

Remember: The mind is lazy. It doesn't want to ramp up attention to absorb a message with a high level of complexity. Simply showing the water resistance of the Samsung S5—or better yet, showing

Competitive Advantage Must Reads

EXPERTS HAVE BEEN DEBATING THE NATURE of competitive advantage for years. Below are four standout articles that articulate the most influential thinking on the subject. They can be found at HBR.org.

"What Is Strategy?" by Michael E. Porter. In this classic 1996 article, Porter argues that operational effectiveness, although necessary to superior performance, is not sufficient, because its techniques are easy to imitate. The essence of strategy is choosing a unique and valuable position rooted in activities that are much more difficult to match.

"The One Number You Need to Grow" by Frederick F. Reichheld. This 2003 article introduced the Net Promoter Score—a simple measure of a customer's willingness to recommend a product. NPS is a reliable index to loyalty, says Reichheld, and the best predictor of top-line growth.

"Transient Advantage" by Rita Gunther McGrath. McGrath contends that business leaders are overly fixated on creating a sustainable competitive advantage. Business today is too turbulent to spend months crafting a long-term strategy, she says in this 2013 article. Rather, leaders need a portfolio of transient advantages that can be built quickly and abandoned just as rapidly.

"When Marketing *Is* Strategy" by Niraj Dawar. For decades, businesses have sought competitive advantage in upstream activities related to making new products—bigger factories, cheaper raw materials, efficiency, and so on. But those are all easily copied. Advantage, says Dawar in this 2013 article, increasingly lies in the marketplace. The important question is not "What else can we make?" but "What else can we do for our customers?"

a customer buying an S5 and being told by the sales rep that it was fully water-resistant—would have been much more powerful. The latter would tell fast thinkers what you wanted them to do: go to a store and buy the Samsung S5. Of course, neither of those ads would be likely to win any awards from marketers focused on the cleverness of advertising copy.

———————

The death of sustainable competitive advantage has been greatly exaggerated. Competitive advantage is as sustainable as it has always been. What is different today is that in a world of infinite communication and innovation, many strategists seem convinced that sustainability can be delivered only by constantly making a company's value proposition the conscious consumer's rational or emotional first choice. They have forgotten, or they never understood, the dominance of the subconscious mind in decision making. For fast thinkers, products and services that are easy to access and that reinforce comfortable buying habits will over time trump innovative but unfamiliar alternatives that may be harder to find and require forming new habits.

So beware of falling into the trap of constantly updating your value proposition and branding. And any company, whether it is a large established player, a niche player, or a new entrant, can sustain the initial advantage provided by a superior value proposition by understanding and following the four rules of cumulative advantage.

Counterpoint

Old Habits Die Hard, but They Do Die

by Rita Gunther McGrath

I love the notion that customers' purchase decisions are more closely related to habit and ease than to loyalty—it brings much-needed insight from behavioral science to the study of consumer decisions. And, as Lafley and Martin suggest, it has major implications for how products are developed and brands are managed. I completely agree with the authors that customers' unconscious minds dominate their decision-making process—and I suspect that any company can benefit from making their routine choices easier, faster, and more convenient. That's one reason the subscription model has become so popular in so many industries—it eliminates the need for customers to consciously decide about routine purchases and offers providers the lure of effortlessly recurring revenue.

The theory of cumulative advantage makes a lot of sense in what Martin Reeves and his colleagues at BCG call a *classical* strategic setting—one in which industry boundaries are clearly delineated, the basis of competition is stable, the environment experiences no major disruptions, and a strong competitive position, once created, can be sustained. As BCG has shown, the candy company Mars has enjoyed very long product life cycles: Snickers and M&M's (introduced in 1930 and 1941, respectively) are among the best-selling candies in the world today. Procter & Gamble has a similarly strong track record with Tide, Unilever with Dove, and PepsiCo with Tropicana orange juice.

But for a growing number of companies, those conditions don't apply. Their industry boundaries aren't clearly delineated—in fact, they're totally blurry. Just ask anyone in retail, entertainment, or telecommunications. Their environments aren't stable—companies can be disrupted by entrants from below, as Clayton Christensen has pointed out, but also by competitors using a different business model or moving over from an adjacent industry. And long-standing competitive strengths can be upended almost overnight by someone who has digitized your physical business (hello, Encyclopaedia Britannica) or turned your product into a service (see Zipcar, Airbnb, and Uber). Apple and Google didn't necessarily *intend* to disrupt point-and-shoot cameras, stand-alone GPS devices, TV advertising, or the Weather Channel, but they did so nonetheless. (See the sidebar "It Works Until It Doesn't: The Changing Nature of Competitive Advantage.")

Strategic Inflection Points

For some time my argument has been that we need a new way of thinking about strategy in environments where traditional barriers to entry are eroding, or in which emerging technologies weaken constraints. Andy Grove's phrase *inflection point* captures this situation nicely. A strategic inflection point, he says, is "a time in the life of a business when its fundamentals are about to change." Inflec-

It Works Until It Doesn't: The Changing Nature of Competitive Advantage

ANY THEORY THAT SEEKS TO explain cause-and-effect relationships operates within a set of constraints. A theory that works beautifully under one set may fall apart under another.

Over the years, we have seen systematic shifts in how companies create a strategically valuable position, often reinforced by the constraints of the systems within which they operate. In the early 1900s, for instance, companies that achieved economies of scope and scale through mass production were dominant, and they remained so right through the period after World War II. Indeed, the *Fortune* 500 list of 1970 reveals the dominance of huge U.S.-based industrial players such as General Motors, General Electric, Exxon Mobil, and Union Carbide.

With the advent of communications and computational technology, strategic advantage began to shift toward companies that leveraged information technology to provide services in addition to goods, and toward models that placed a value on information utilization in addition to product features and functions. Although the industrial giants remained in place for a long time, companies such as Walmart, AIG, Enron, and Citigroup had joined them on the *Fortune* 500 list by 1995.

Today the dynamics of competitive advantage have shifted once more. Companies are achieving advantage through *access* to assets rather than ownership of them. In addition, a whole new category of "platform" companies, such as Google, Apple, and Facebook, have emerged, and the very size of their customer base creates a reinforcing virtuous cycle. Often called network effects, these dynamics mean that the more customers a company has, the more valuable it is to each additional customer. In such cases being an early mover can result in a formidable advantage.

The point is that every theory has its constraints. Attempting to apply it outside those conditions can lead to disaster.

---

tion points are difficult for traditional strategy tools to address, because they usually don't look important at first. The Wright brothers proved it was possible to fly safely in 1903. Nobody took that seriously until 1908. Even with the 1914 launch of the first commercial flight, few realized that airplanes would upend industries as varied as railroads, steamships, and package delivery.

Consumer habits can be powerful aids to sustaining a competitive advantage, as Lafley and Martin quite correctly point out. But habits, like other elements of the environment, can change. And when new technologies make new business models viable, habits can change very fast.

Consider the powerful forces that were unleashed from 2004 to 2007 by four separate but linked business developments. In 2004 Facebook was founded. In 2005 YouTube was founded. In 2006 Amazon launched Amazon Web Services (AWS). In 2007 Apple's iPhone and Google's Android operating system were commercially released. As the technology analyst Ben Thompson points out, AWS made it easy and cheap to start an online company, YouTube made it easy and cheap to upload videos, and Facebook offered a ready-made channel for sharing such videos. I'd add that the wild popularity of mobile phones made all that available to ordinary people. Now a couple of guys with an idea and access to programming skills can rival global giants in days or weeks, not months or years—with practically no assets.

Gillette Versus Dollar Shave

And that's exactly what happened with the 2012 launch of DollarShaveClub.com. The brand promise was simple: great razors with few frills, for a low subscription price, delivered to your door automatically. Not only did you save money, but you didn't have to visit a store or risk running out. This was all the more attractive because habitual buying behavior had already been disrupted: Razor blades are expensive and easy to steal, so it has become common for them to be kept under lock and key in stores. Today, although Dollar Shave Club has an 8% share of the $3 billion U.S. market for blades and razors, the far more important number is its "share of cartridge." That, according to recent sources, is an astonishing 15% of all cartridges sold.

In 2010 Gillette had 70% of the global shaving market and legions of loyal customers who reliably traded up as the next generation of products, with higher prices, were released. Procter & Gamble had acquired the brand in 2005 for a reported $57 billion. It was a classic high-market-share, high-quality business—and we can only assume from their track records that both Gillette and P&G were extremely good at getting customers to buy habitually. Clearly they had a strong cumulative advantage. But that wasn't enough, because the business had hit an inflection point.

In July 2016 Unilever agreed to buy Dollar Shave Club for about $1 billion in cash. The founding entrepreneurs are happy. Their investors are happy. Their customers are clearly happy. The incumbents? Not so much. According to the *Wall Street Journal,* P&G's share of men's razors and blades had fallen to 59% in 2015. One of its responses was to launch the Gillette Shave Club. Having seen the potentially habit-destroying effects of the subscription model, P&G now offers subscription and delivery for other products—including expensive Tide Pods.

Twenty years ago it would have been inconceivable that a marketing message could reach 20 million people in a matter of weeks without massive spending on television and other advertising. But Dollar Shave Club accomplished that with an entertaining launch video, promotion on social media channels, and a group of enthusiastic brand ambassadors who provided feet on the ground to promote its products—free.

Leveraging the Familiar Even as You Reinvent

The point of this story is that even a company as storied as P&G can be taken by surprise. Which brings me to the tricky question, How can executives balance the formidable power of cumulative advantage and habit, often associated with a brand, with the need to refresh their approach?

One practical tactic is to leverage the core skills or capabilities of an organization in a new format. Target offers an illustrative case. The company's roots were in a traditional department store, Dayton's, which became Dayton Hudson and eventually Marshall Field's. In 1960 its leadership saw an opportunity to reach a market segment that appeared to be growing but wasn't well served by the existing format. That segment consisted of value-conscious consumers who nonetheless appreciated good design and a reasonably pleasant shopping experience. To protect the then-dominant department store brand, the new venture was branded separately. Its iconic bull's-eye logo was meant to represent the notion of hitting the target of convenience, price, and customer experience.

By the mid-1970s Target stores were outselling the company's department stores. In 2000 Dayton Hudson changed its name to Target to reflect the reality of its now-core business. In 2004 the company sold its department store brands, completing an extraordinary retail transformation.

Another fascinating transformation that leveraged the core skills of a parent company is the relentless digitization pursued by the newspaper publisher Schibsted, of Norway. Unlike many other newspaper publishers, Schibsted saw the encroachment of digital classified advertisements as an opportunity rather than a threat to its business. Beginning in the late 1990s, its leaders aggressively courted classified advertisers to list with its digital properties. This became a crusade. As Sverre Munck observed when he was the EVP for strategy and international editorial, "The Internet was made for classifieds and classifieds were made for the Internet." Long a traditional media company, Schibsted was able to leverage deep ties with its advertisers with a model that permitted economies of scale in editorial and communication activities across its media brands. These were supplemented by a significant commitment to bringing technological capabilities into the very core of the media business, ending the tug-of-war between conventional editorial processes and the logic of digital transformation.

A Balance of Stability and Dynamism

In 2012 I wrote an HBR piece titled "How the Growth Outliers Do It." That analysis, which looked at 10 years of net income data from 2000 to 2009, found that out of 2,347 of the publicly traded firms with a market capitalization of more than $1 billion, only 10 had successfully grown net income by 5% or more in every one of those 10 years.

(Although performance can be measured in many ways, this seems to me to be one that tests the idea of sustainable advantage consistently.) The first conclusion is obvious: Steady, sustained profit growth is hard to achieve, particularly in a period that includes the Great Recession of 2008. The second, however, is that some companies do manage to achieve it for relatively long periods of time. I found that those companies balanced elements of stability (culture, relationships, leadership, and even strategy) with elements of dynamism (rapid resource mobilization, marketplace experiments, and people mobility).

I spoke recently with Malcolm Frank, a senior executive at Cognizant, which appears on both my original list and one that I've updated through the end of 2015 (for which I used modified criteria: If a company was over the threshold for any year in the previous 10 years, it was included on the list, which totaled roughly 5,300). Frank told me that his organization lives and breathes the idea that in many cases competitive advantage is not going to last. "For us, what was the ceiling five years ago is going to be the floor five years from now," he said. Cognizant is also disciplined about exiting slow-growth or underperforming operations. But it is remarkably stable. Francisco D'Souza has been CEO since 2007, and the most recent addition to the leadership team joined in 2005. Cognizant's culture, too, reflects what its leaders call a "well-established set of cultural values," as demonstrated in their written documents, public statements, and go-to-market strategies.

But let's return to the really important insight that underlies the argument of Lafley and Martin: Most of the time, we are all unaware of the true motivations behind the choices we make. The better strategists and marketers become at understanding those motivations, the more likely they are to succeed at building habitual behavior among consumers—and, just as important, the more likely they are to see how those habits might change. Clayton Christensen's "jobs to be done" theory may come in handy here. He has famously said that when we buy products, we are actually hiring them to do a job for us. And the "jobs" underlying most product purchases are re-markably stable. Take communication: From smoke signals to the Pony Express to the telegraph to the telephone to the communications technologies of today, our basic job—to send messages to other human beings—has not changed. But how that job gets done has changed dramatically. If incumbent companies stay focused on the job itself—rather than on the specifics of how it gets done at this moment in time—they may be able to invent a better way before the competition does.

This is a point that company leaders often miss. Customers can easily "hire" another solution that does a given job better—just as vast numbers of them are currently doing with razors bought by subscription.

Originally published in January–February 2017. Reprint R1701B

Noise

How to Overcome the High, Hidden Cost of
Inconsistent Decision Making. *by Daniel Kahneman,
Andrew M. Rosenfield, Linnea Gandhi, and Tom Blaser*

AT A GLOBAL FINANCIAL SERVICES FIRM we worked with, a longtime customer accidentally submitted the same application file to two offices. Though the employees who reviewed the file were supposed to follow the same guidelines—and thus arrive at similar outcomes—the separate offices returned very different quotes. Taken aback, the customer gave the business to a competitor. From the point of view of the firm, employees in the same role should have been interchangeable, but in this case they were not. Unfortunately, this is a common problem.

Professionals in many organizations are assigned arbitrarily to cases: appraisers in credit-rating agencies, physicians in emergency rooms, underwriters of loans and insurance, and others. Organizations expect consistency from these professionals: Identical cases should be treated similarly, if not identically. The problem is that humans are unreliable decision makers; their judgments are strongly influenced by irrelevant factors, such as their current mood, the time since their last meal, and the weather. We call the chance variability of judgments *noise.* It is an invisible tax on the bottom line of many companies.

Some jobs are noise-free. Clerks at a bank or a post office perform complex tasks, but they must follow strict rules that limit subjective judgment and guarantee, by design, that identical cases will be treated identically. In contrast, medical professionals, loan officers, project managers, judges, and executives all make judgment calls, which are guided by informal experience and general principles rather than by rigid rules. And if they don't reach precisely the same answer that every other person in their role would, that's acceptable; this is what we mean when we say that a decision is "a matter of judgment." A firm whose employees exercise judgment does not expect decisions to be entirely free of noise. But often noise is *far above* the level that executives would consider tolerable—and they are completely unaware of it.

The prevalence of noise has been demonstrated in several studies. Academic researchers have repeatedly confirmed that professionals often contradict their own prior judgments when given the same data on different occasions. For instance, when software developers were asked on two separate days to estimate the completion time for a given task, the hours they projected differed by 71%, on average. When pathologists made two assessments of the severity of biopsy results, the correlation between their ratings was only .61 (out of a perfect 1.0), indicating that they made inconsistent diagnoses quite frequently. Judgments made by different people are even more likely to diverge. Research has confirmed that in many tasks, experts' decisions are highly variable: valuing stocks, appraising real estate, sentencing criminals, evaluating job performance, auditing financial statements, and more. The unavoidable conclusion is that professionals often make decisions that deviate significantly from those of their peers, from their own prior decisions, and from rules that they themselves claim to follow.

Noise is often insidious: It causes even successful companies to lose substantial amounts of money without realizing it. How substantial? To get an estimate, we asked executives in one of the organizations we studied the following: "Suppose the optimal assessment of a case is $100,000. What would be the cost to the organization if the professional in charge of the case assessed a value of $115,000? What would be the cost of assessing it at $85,000?" The cost estimates were high. Aggregated over the assessments made every year, the cost of noise was measured in billions—an unacceptable number

Idea in Brief

The Problem

Many organizations expect consistency from their professional employees. However, human judgment is often influenced by such irrelevant factors as the weather and the last case seen. More important, decisions often vary from employee to employee. The chance variability of judgments is called *noise,* and it is surprisingly costly to companies.

The Starting Point

Managers should perform a noise audit in which members of a unit, working independently, evaluate a common set of cases. The degree to which their decisions vary is the measure of noise. It will often be dramatically higher than executives anticipate.

The Solution

The most radical solution to a severe noise problem is to replace human judgment with algorithms. Algorithms are not difficult to construct—but often they're politically or operationally infeasible. In such instances, companies should establish procedures to help professionals achieve greater consistency.

even for a large global firm. The value of reducing noise even by a few percentage points would be in the tens of millions. Remarkably, the organization had completely ignored the question of consistency until then.

It has long been known that predictions and decisions generated by simple statistical algorithms are often more accurate than those made by experts, even when the experts have access to more information than the formulas use. It is less well known that the key advantage of algorithms is that they are noise-free: Unlike humans, a formula will always return the same output for any given input. Superior consistency allows even simple and imperfect algorithms to achieve greater accuracy than human professionals. (Of course, there are times when algorithms will be operationally or politically infeasible, as we will discuss.)

In this article we explain the difference between noise and bias and look at how executives can audit the level and impact of noise in their organizations. We then describe an inexpensive, underused method for building algorithms that remediate noise, and we sketch out procedures that can promote consistency when algorithms are not an option.

Noise vs. Bias

When people consider errors in judgment and decision making, they most likely think of social biases like the stereotyping of minorities or of cognitive biases such as overconfidence and unfounded optimism. The useless variability that we call noise is a different type of error. To appreciate the distinction, think of your bathroom scale. We would say that the scale is *biased* if its readings are generally either too high or too low. If your weight appears to depend on where you happen to place your feet, the scale is *noisy.* A scale that consistently underestimates true weight by exactly four pounds is seriously biased but free of noise. A scale that gives two different readings when you step on it twice is noisy. Many errors of measurement arise from a combination of bias and noise. Most inexpensive bathroom scales are somewhat biased and quite noisy.

For a visual illustration of the distinction, consider the targets in the exhibit "How noise and bias affect accuracy." These show the results of target practice for four-person teams in which each individual shoots once.

- Team A is *accurate:* The shots of the teammates are on the bull's-eye and close to one another.

- The other three teams are inaccurate but in distinctive ways:

- Team B is *noisy:* The shots of its members are centered around the bull's-eye but widely scattered.

- Team C is *biased:* The shots all missed the bull's-eye but cluster together.

- Team D is both *noisy* and *biased.*

As a comparison of teams A and B illustrates, an increase in noise always impairs accuracy when there is no bias. When bias is present, increasing noise may actually cause a lucky hit, as happened for

How noise and bias affect accuracy

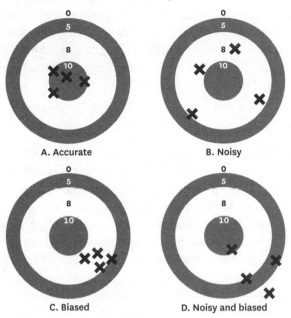

A. Accurate   B. Noisy

C. Biased   D. Noisy and biased

team D. Of course, no organization would put its trust in luck. Noise is always undesirable—and sometimes disastrous.

It is obviously useful to an organization to know about bias and noise in the decisions of its employees, but collecting that information isn't straightforward. Different issues arise in measuring these errors. A major problem is that the outcomes of decisions often aren't known until far in the future, if at all. Loan officers, for example, frequently must wait several years to see how loans they approved worked out, and they almost never know what happens to an applicant they reject.

Unlike bias, noise can be measured without knowing what an accurate response would be. To illustrate, imagine that the targets at which the shooters aimed were erased from the exhibit. You would know nothing about the teams' overall accuracy, but you could be certain that something was wrong with the scattered shots of teams B and D: Wherever the bull's-eye was, they did not all come close to hitting it. All that's required to measure noise in judgments is a simple experiment in which a few realistic cases are evaluated independently by several professionals. Here again, the scattering of judgments can be observed without knowing the correct answer. We call such experiments *noise audits*.

Performing a Noise Audit

The point of a noise audit is not to produce a report. The ultimate goal is to improve the quality of decisions, and an audit can be successful only if the leaders of the unit are prepared to accept unpleasant results and act on them. Such buy-in is easier to achieve if the executives view the study as their own creation. To that end, the cases should be compiled by respected team members and should cover the range of problems typically encountered. To make the results relevant to everyone, all unit members should participate in the audit. A social scientist with experience in conducting rigorous behavioral experiments should supervise the technical aspects of the audit, but the professional unit must own the process.

Recently, we helped two financial services organizations conduct noise audits. The duties and expertise of the two groups we studied were quite different, but both required the evaluation of moderately complex materials and often involved decisions about hundreds of thousands of dollars. We followed the same protocol in both organizations. First we asked managers of the professional teams involved to construct several realistic case files for evaluation. To prevent information about the experiment from leaking, the entire exercise was conducted on the same day. Employees were asked to spend about half the day analyzing two to four cases. They were to decide on a dollar amount for each, as in their normal routine. To avoid collusion, the participants were not told that the study was concerned with reliability. In one organization, for example, the goals were described as understanding the employees' professional thinking, increasing their tools' usefulness, and improving communication among colleagues. About 70 professionals in organization A participated, and about 50 in organization B.

We constructed a noise index for each case, which answered the following question: "By how much do the judgments of two randomly chosen employees differ?" We expressed this amount as a percentage of their average. Suppose the assessments of a case by two employees are $600 and $1,000. The average of their assessments is $800, and the difference between them is $400, so the noise index is 50% for this pair. We performed the same computation for all pairs of employees and then calculated an overall average noise index for each case.

Pre-audit interviews with executives in the two organizations indicated that they expected the differences between their professionals' decisions to range from 5% to 10%—a level they considered acceptable for "matters of judgment." The results came as a shock. The noise index ranged from 34% to 62% for the six cases in organization A, and the overall average was 48%. In the four cases in organization B, the noise index ranged from 46% to 70%, with an average of 60%. Perhaps most disappointing, experience on the job did not appear to reduce noise. Among professionals with five or more years on the job, average disagreement was 46% in organization A and 62% in organization B.

No one had seen this coming. But because they owned the study, the executives in both organizations accepted the conclusion that the judgments of their professionals were unreliable to an extent that could not be tolerated. All quickly agreed that something had to be done to control the problem.

Because the findings were consistent with prior research on the low reliability of professional judgment, they didn't surprise us. The major puzzle for us was the fact that neither organization had ever considered reliability to be an issue.

The problem of noise is effectively invisible in the business world; we have observed that audiences are quite surprised when the reliability of professional judgment is mentioned as an issue. What prevents companies from recognizing that the judgments of their employees are noisy? The answer lies in two familiar phenomena:

Experienced professionals tend to have high confidence in the accuracy of their own judgments, and they also have high regard for their colleagues' intelligence. This combination inevitably leads to an overestimation of agreement. When asked about what their colleagues would say, professionals expect others' judgments to be much closer to their own than they actually are. Most of the time, of course, experienced professionals are completely unconcerned with what others might think and simply assume that theirs is the best answer. One reason the problem of noise is invisible is that people do not go through life imagining plausible alternatives to every judgment they make.

The expectation that others will agree with you is sometimes justified, particularly where judgments are so skilled that they are intuitive. High-level chess and driving are standard examples of tasks that have been practiced to near perfection. Master players who look at a situation on a chessboard will all have very similar assessments of the state of the game—whether, say, the white queen is in danger or black's king-side defense is weak. The same is true of drivers. Negotiating traffic would be impossibly dangerous if we could not assume that the drivers around us share our understanding of priorities at intersections and roundabouts. There is little or no noise at high levels of skill.

High skill develops in chess and driving through years of practice in a predictable environment, in which actions are followed by feedback that is both immediate and clear. Unfortunately, few professionals operate in such a world. In most jobs people learn to make judgments by hearing managers and colleagues explain and criticize—a much less reliable source of knowledge than learning from one's mistakes. Long experience on a job always increases people's confidence in their judgments, but in the absence of rapid feedback, confidence is no guarantee of either accuracy or consensus.

We offer this aphorism in summary: *Where there is judgment, there is noise—and usually more of it than you think.* As a rule, we believe that neither professionals nor their managers can make a good guess about the reliability of their judgments. The only way to get an accurate assessment is to conduct a noise audit. And at least in some cases, the problem will be severe enough to require action.

Types of noise and bias

Bias and noise are distinct kinds of error. Each comes in different variants and requires different corrective actions.

Type of bias	Examples	Corrective actions
General The average judgment is wrong.	• Planning fallacy: Forecasts of outcomes are mostly optimistic • Excessive risk aversion: A venture capital firm rejects too many promising but risky investments	• Continual monitoring of decisions • Guidelines and targets for the frequency of certain outcomes (such as loan approvals) • Eliminating incentives that favor biases
Social Discrimination occurs against—or for—certain categories of cases.	• Frequent denial of credit to qualified applicants from certain ethnic groups • Gender bias in assessments of job performance	• Monitoring statistics for different groups • Blinding of applications • Objective and quantifiable metrics • Open channels for complaints • Guidelines and training
Cognitive Decisions are strongly influenced by irrelevant factors or insensitive to relevant ones.	• Excessive effects of first impressions • Effects of anchors (such as an opening offer in negotiation) • Myopic neglect of future consequences	• Training employees to detect situations in which biases are likely to occur • Critiques of important decisions, focused on likely biases

Type of noise	Examples	Corrective actions
Variability across occasions Decisions vary when the same case is presented more than once to the same individual.	• A hiring officer's judgments of a file are influenced by her mood or the quality of the previous applicant	• Algorithms to replace human judgment • Checklists that encourage a consistent approach to decisions
Variability across individuals Professionals in the same role make different decisions.	• Some individuals are generally more lenient than others • Some individuals are more cautious than others	• Algorithms to replace human judgment • Frequent monitoring of individuals' decisions • Roundtables at which differences are explored and resolved • Checklists that encourage a consistent approach to decisions

Dialing Down the Noise

The most radical solution to the noise problem is to replace human judgment with formal rules—known as algorithms—that use the data about a case to produce a prediction or a decision. People have competed against algorithms in several hundred contests of accuracy over the past 60 years, in tasks ranging from predicting the life expectancy of cancer patients to predicting the success of graduate students. Algorithms were more accurate than human professionals in about half the studies, and approximately tied with the humans in the others. The ties should also count as victories for the algorithms, which are more cost-effective.

In many situations, of course, algorithms will not be practical. The application of a rule may not be feasible when inputs are idiosyncratic or hard to code in a consistent format. Algorithms are also less likely to be useful for judgments or decisions that involve multiple dimensions or depend on negotiation with another party. Even when an algorithmic solution is available in principle, organizational considerations sometimes prevent implementation. The replacement of existing employees by software is a painful process that will encounter resistance unless it frees those employees up for more-enjoyable tasks.

But if the conditions are right, developing and implementing algorithms can be surprisingly easy. The common assumption is that algorithms require statistical analysis of large amounts of data. For example, most people we talk to believe that data on thousands of loan applications and their outcomes is needed to develop an equation that predicts commercial loan defaults. Very few know that adequate algorithms can be developed without any outcome data at all—and with input information on only a small number of cases. We call predictive formulas that are built without outcome data "reasoned rules," because they draw on commonsense reasoning.

The construction of a reasoned rule starts with the selection of a few (perhaps six to eight) variables that are incontrovertibly related to the outcome being predicted. If the outcome is loan default, for example, assets and liabilities will surely be included in the list. The

How to Build a Reasoned Rule

YOU DON'T NEED OUTCOME DATA to create useful predictive algorithms. For example, you can build a reasoned rule that predicts loan defaults quite effectively without knowing what happened to past loans; all you need is a small set of recent loan applications. Here are the next steps:

1. Select six to eight variables that are distinct and obviously related to the predicted outcome. Assets and revenues (weighted positively) and liabilities (weighted negatively) would surely be included, along with a few other features of loan applications.

2. Take the data from your set of cases (all the loan applications from the past year) and compute the mean and standard deviation of each variable in that set.

3. For every case in the set, compute a "standard score" for each variable: the difference between the value in the case and the mean of the whole set, divided by the standard deviation. With standard scores, all variables are expressed on the same scale and can be compared and averaged.

4. Compute a "summary score" for each case—the average of its variables' standard scores. This is the output of the reasoned rule. The same formula will be used for new cases, using the mean and standard deviation of the original set and updating periodically.

5. Order the cases in the set from high to low summary scores, and determine the appropriate actions for different ranges of scores. With loan applications, for instance, the actions might be "the top 10% of applicants will receive a discount" and "the bottom 30% will be turned down."

You are now ready to apply the rule to new cases. The algorithm will compute a summary score for each new case and generate a decision.

---

next step is to assign these variables equal weight in the prediction formula, setting their sign in the obvious direction (positive for assets, negative for liabilities). The rule can then be constructed by a few simple calculations. (For more details, see the sidebar "How to Build a Reasoned Rule.")

The surprising result of much research is that in many contexts reasoned rules are about as accurate as statistical models built with outcome data. Standard statistical models combine a set of predictive variables, which are assigned weights based on their relationship to the predicted outcomes and to one another. In many situations, however, these weights are both statistically unstable and practically unimportant. A simple rule that assigns equal weights to the selected variables is likely to be just as valid. Algorithms that weight variables equally and don't rely on outcome data have proved successful in personnel selection, election forecasting, predictions about football games, and other applications.

The bottom line here is that if you plan to use an algorithm to reduce noise, you need not wait for outcome data. You can reap most of the benefits by using common sense to select variables and the simplest possible rule to combine them.

Of course, no matter what type of algorithm is employed, people must retain ultimate control. Algorithms must be monitored and adjusted for occasional changes in the population of cases. Managers must also keep an eye on individual decisions and have the authority to override the algorithm in clear-cut cases. For example, a decision to approve a loan should be provisionally reversed if the firm discovers that the applicant has been arrested. Most important, executives should determine how to translate the algorithm's output into action. The algorithm can tell you which prospective loans are in the top 5% or in the bottom 10% of all applications, but someone must decide what to do with that information.

Algorithms are sometimes used as an intermediate source of information for professionals, who make the final decisions. One example is the Public Safety Assessment, a formula that was developed to help U.S. judges decide whether a defendant can be safely released pending trial. In its first six months of use in Kentucky, crime among defendants on pretrial release fell by about 15%, while the percentage of people released pretrial increased. It's obvious in this case that human judges must retain the final authority for the decisions: The public would be shocked to see justice meted out by a formula.

Uncomfortable as people may be with the idea, studies have shown that while humans can provide useful input to formulas, algorithms do better in the role of final decision maker. If the avoidance of errors is the only criterion, managers should be strongly advised to overrule the algorithm only in exceptional circumstances.

Bringing Discipline to Judgment

Replacing human decisions with an algorithm should be considered whenever professional judgments are noisy, but in most cases this solution will be too radical or simply impractical. An alternative is to adopt procedures that promote consistency by ensuring that employees in the same role use similar methods to seek information, integrate it into a view of the case, and translate that view into a decision. A thorough examination of everything required to do that is beyond the scope of this article, but we can offer some basic advice, with the important caveat that instilling discipline in judgment is not at all easy.

Training is crucial, of course, but even professionals who were trained together tend to drift into their own way of doing things. Firms sometimes combat drift by organizing roundtables at which decision makers gather to review cases. Unfortunately, most roundtables are run in a way that makes it much too easy to achieve agreement, because participants quickly converge on the opinions stated first or most confidently. To prevent such spurious agreement, the individual participants in a roundtable should study the case independently, form opinions they're prepared to defend, and send those opinions to the group leader before the meeting. Such roundtables will effectively provide an audit of noise, with the added step of a group discussion in which differences of opinion are explored.

As an alternative or addition to roundtables, professionals should be offered user-friendly tools, such as checklists and carefully formulated questions, to guide them as they collect information about a case, make intermediate judgments, and formulate a final decision. Unwanted variability occurs at each of those stages, and firms can—and should—test how much such tools reduce it. Ideally, the people who use these tools will view them as aids that help them do their jobs effectively and economically. Unfortunately, our experience suggests that the task of constructing judgment tools that are both effective and user-friendly is more difficult than many executives think. Controlling noise is hard, but we expect that an organization that conducts an audit and evaluates the cost of noise in dollars will conclude that reducing random variability is worth the effort.

Our main goal in this article is to introduce managers to the concept of noise as a source of errors and explain how it is distinct from bias. The term "bias" has entered the public consciousness to the extent that the words "error" and "bias" are often used interchangeably. In fact, better decisions are not achieved merely by reducing general biases (such as optimism) or specific social and cognitive biases (such as discrimination against women or anchoring effects). Executives who are concerned with accuracy should also confront the prevalence of inconsistency in professional judgments. Noise is more difficult to appreciate than bias, but it is no less real or less costly.

Originally published in October 2016. Reprint R1610B

Visualizations That Really Work

by Scott Berinato

NOT LONG AGO, THE ABILITY to create smart data visualizations, or dataviz, was a nice-to-have skill. For the most part, it benefited design- and data-minded managers who made a deliberate decision to invest in acquiring it. That's changed. Now visual communication is a must-have skill for all managers, because more and more often, it's the only way to make sense of the work they do.

Data is the primary force behind this shift. Decision making increasingly relies on data, which comes at us with such overwhelming velocity, and in such volume, that we can't comprehend it without some layer of abstraction, such as a visual one. A typical example: At Boeing the managers of the Osprey program need to improve the efficiency of the aircraft's takeoffs and landings. But each time the Osprey gets off the ground or touches back down, its sensors create a terabyte of data. Ten takeoffs and landings produce as much data as is held in the Library of Congress. Without visualization, detecting the inefficiencies hidden in the patterns and anomalies of that data would be an impossible slog.

But even information that's not statistical demands visual expression. Complex systems—business process workflows, for example, or the way customers move through a store—are hard to understand, much less fix, if you can't first see them.

Thanks to the internet and a growing number of affordable tools, translating information into visuals is now easy (and cheap) for everyone, regardless of data skills or design skills. This is largely a positive development. One drawback, though, is that it reinforces the impulse to "click and viz" without first thinking about your purpose and goals. *Convenient* is a tempting replacement for good, but it will lead to charts that are merely adequate or, worse, ineffective. Automatically converting spreadsheet cells into a chart only visualizes pieces of a spreadsheet; it doesn't capture an idea. As the presentation expert Nancy Duarte puts it, "Don't project the idea that you're showing a chart. Project the idea that you're showing a reflection of human activity, of things people did to make a line go up and down. It's not 'Here are our Q3 financial results,' it's 'Here's where we missed our targets.'"

Managers who want to get better at making charts often start by learning rules. When should I use a bar chart? How many colors are too many? Where should the key go? Do I have to start my y-axis at zero? Visual grammar is important and useful—but knowing it doesn't guarantee that you'll make good charts. To start with chart-making rules is to forgo strategy for execution; it's to pack for a trip without knowing where you're going.

Your visual communication will prove far more successful if you begin by acknowledging that it is not a lone action but, rather, several activities, each of which requires distinct types of planning, resources, and skills. The typology I offer here was created as a reaction to my making the very mistake I just described: The book from which this article is adapted started out as something like a rule book. But after exploring the history of visualization, the exciting state of visualization research, and smart ideas from experts and pioneers, I reconsidered the project. We didn't need another rule book; we needed a way to think about the increasingly crucial discipline of visual communication as a whole.

The typology described in this article is simple. By answering just two questions, you can set yourself up to succeed.

The Two Questions

To start thinking visually, consider the nature and purpose of your visualization:

Is the information *conceptual* or *data-driven*?

Am I *declaring* something or *exploring* something?

Idea in Brief

Context

Knowledge workers need greater visual literacy than they used to, because so much data—and so many ideas—are now presented graphically. But few of us have been taught data-visualization skills.

Tools are fine . . .

Inexpensive tools allow anyone to perform simple tasks such as importing spreadsheet data into a bar chart. But that means it's easy to create terrible charts. Visualization can be so much more: It's an agile, powerful way to explore ideas and communicate information.

. . . But strategy is key

Don't jump straight to execution. Instead, first think about what you're representing—ideas or data? Then consider your purpose: Do you want to inform, persuade, or explore? The answers will suggest what tools and resources you need.

If you know the answers to these questions, you can plan what resources and tools you'll need and begin to discern what type of visualization will help you achieve your goals most effectively.

	Conceptual	Data-driven
Focus	*Ideas*	*Statistics*
Goals	*Simplify, teach* "Here's how our organization is structured."	*Inform, enlighten* "Here are our revenues for the past two years."

The first question is the simpler of the two, and the answer is usually obvious. Either you're visualizing qualitative information or you're plotting quantitative information: ideas or statistics. But notice that the question is about the information itself, not the forms you might ultimately use to show it. For example, the classic Gartner Hype Cycle (see following page) uses a traditionally data-driven form—a line chart—but no actual data. It's a concept.

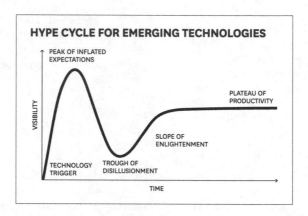

HYPE CYCLE FOR EMERGING TECHNOLOGIES

If the first question identifies what you *have*, the second elicits what you're *doing*: either communicating information (declarative) or trying to figure something out (exploratory).

	Declarative	Exploratory
Focus	*Documenting, designing*	*Prototyping, iterating, interacting, automating*
Goals	*Affirm* "Here is our budget by department."	*Confirm* "Let's see if marketing investments contributed to rising profits." *Discover* "What would we see if we visualized customer purchases by gender, location, and purchase amount in real time?"

Managers most often work with declarative visualizations, which make a statement, usually to an audience in a formal setting. If you have a spreadsheet workbook full of sales data and you're using it to show quarterly sales in a presentation, your purpose is declarative.

But let's say your boss wants to understand why the sales team's performance has lagged lately. You suspect that seasonal cycles have caused the dip, but you're not sure. Now your purpose is exploratory, and you'll use the same data to create visuals that will confirm or refute your hypothesis. The audience is usually yourself or a small team. If your hypothesis is confirmed, you may well show your boss a declarative visualization, saying, "Here's what's happening to sales."

Exploratory visualizations are actually of two kinds. In the example above, you were testing a hypothesis. But suppose you don't have an idea about why performance is lagging—you don't know what you're looking for. You want to mine your workbook to see what patterns, trends, and anomalies emerge. What will you see, for example, when you measure sales performance in relation to the size of the region a salesperson manages? What happens if you compare seasonal trends in various geographies? How does weather affect sales? Such data brainstorming can deliver fresh insights. Big strategic questions—Why are revenues falling? Where can we find efficiencies? How do customers interact with us?—can benefit from a discovery-focused exploratory visualization.

The Four Types

The nature and purpose questions combine in a classic 2×2 to define four types of visual communication: idea illustration, idea generation, visual discovery, and everyday dataviz.

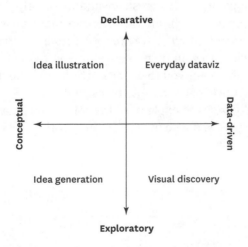

Idea illustration

Info type	Process, framework
Typical setting	Presentations, teaching
Primary skills	Design, editing
Goals	Learning, simplifying, explaining

We might call this quadrant the "consultants' corner." Consultants can't resist process diagrams, cycle diagrams, and the like. At their best, idea illustrations clarify complex ideas by drawing on our ability to understand metaphors (trees, bridges) and simple design conventions (circles, hierarchies). Org charts and decision trees are classic examples of idea illustration. So is the 2×2 that frames this article.

Idea illustration demands clear and simple design, but its reliance on metaphor invites unnecessary adornment. Because the discipline and boundaries of data sets aren't built in to idea illustration, they must be imposed. The focus should be on clear communication, structure, and the logic of the ideas. The most useful skills here are similar to what a text editor brings to a manuscript—the ability to pare things down to their essence. Some design skills will be useful too, whether they're your own or hired.

Suppose a company engages consultants to help its R&D group find inspiration in other industries. The consultants use a technique called the *pyramid search*—a way to get information from experts in other fields close to your own, who point you to the top experts in their fields, who point you to experts in still other fields, who then help you find the experts in those fields, and so on.

It's actually tricky to explain, so the consultants may use visualization to help. How does a pyramid search work? It looks something like this:

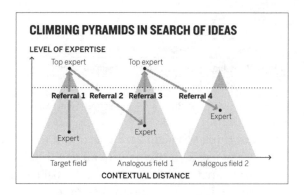

The axes use conventions that we can grasp immediately: industries plotted near to far and expertise mapped low to high. The pyramid shape itself shows the relative rarity of top experts compared with lower-level ones. Words in the title—"climbing" and "pyramids"—help us grasp the idea quickly. Finally, the designer didn't succumb to a temptation to decorate: The pyramids aren't literal, three-dimensional, sandstone-colored objects.

Too often, idea illustration doesn't go that well, and you end up with something like this:

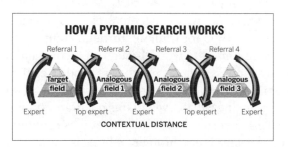

Here the color gradient, the drop shadows, and the 3-D pyramids distract us from the idea. The arrows don't actually demonstrate how a pyramid search works. And experts and top experts are placed on the same plane instead of at different heights to convey relative status.

Idea generation

Info type	Complex, undefined
Typical setting	Working session, brainstorming
Primary skills	Team-building, facilitation
Goals	Problem solving, discovery, innovation

Managers may not think of visualization as a tool to support idea generation, but they use it to brainstorm all the time—on whiteboards, on butcher paper, or, classically, on the back of a napkin. Like idea illustration, idea generation relies on conceptual metaphors, but it takes place in more-informal settings, such as off-sites, strategy sessions, and early-phase innovation projects. It's used to find new ways of seeing how the business works and to answer complex managerial challenges: restructuring an organization, coming up with a new business process, codifying a system for making decisions.

Although idea generation can be done alone, it benefits from collaboration and borrows from design thinking—gathering as many diverse points of view and visual approaches as possible before homing in on one and refining it. Jon Kolko, the founder and director of the Austin Center for Design and the author of *Well-Designed: How to Use Empathy to Create Products People Love,* fills the whiteboard walls of his office with conceptual, exploratory visualizations. "It's our go-to method for thinking through complexity," he says. "Sketching is this effort to work through ambiguity and muddiness and come to crispness." Managers who are good at leading teams, facilitating brainstorming sessions, and encouraging and then capturing creative thinking will do well in this quadrant. Design skills and editing are less important here, and sometimes counterproductive. When you're seeking breakthroughs, editing is the opposite of what you need, and you should think in rapid sketches; refined designs will just slow you down.

Suppose a marketing team is holding an off-site. The team members need to come up with a way to show executives their proposed strategy for going upmarket. An hourlong whiteboard session yields several approaches and ideas (none of which are erased) for presenting the strategy. Ultimately, one approach gains purchase with the team, which thinks it best captures the key point: Get fewer customers to spend much more. The whiteboard looks something like this:

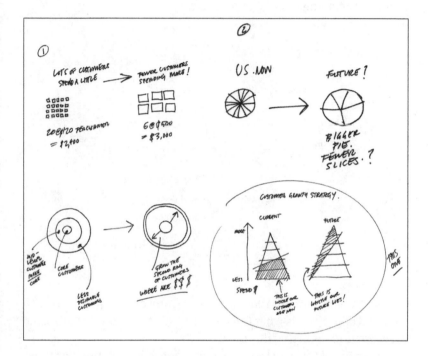

Of course, visuals that emerge from idea generation often lead to more formally designed and presented idea illustrations.

Visual discovery

Info type	Big data, complex, dynamic
Typical setting	Working sessions, testing, analysis
Primary skills	Business intelligence, programming, paired analysis
Goals	Trend spotting, sense making, deep analysis

This is the most complicated quadrant, because in truth it holds two categories. Recall that we originally separated exploratory purposes into two kinds: testing a hypothesis and mining for patterns, trends, and anomalies. The former is focused, whereas the latter is more flexible. The bigger and more complex the data, and the less you know going in, the more open-ended the work.

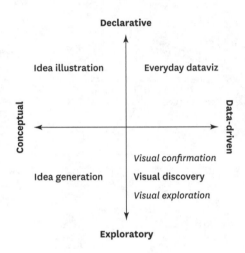

Visual Confirmation. You're answering one of two questions with this kind of project: Is what I suspect actually true? or What are some other ways of depicting this idea?

The scope of the data tends to be manageable, and the chart types you're likely to use are common—although when trying to depict things in new ways, you may venture into some less-common types. Confirmation usually doesn't happen in a formal setting; it's the work you do to find the charts you want to create for presentations. That means your time will shift away from design and toward proto-typing that allows you to rapidly iterate on the dataviz. Some skill at manipulating spreadsheets and knowledge of programs or sites that enable swift prototyping are useful here.

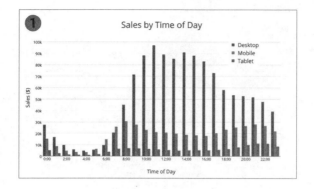

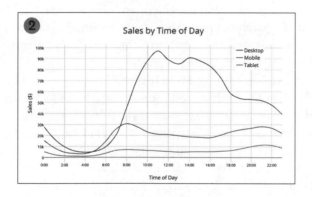

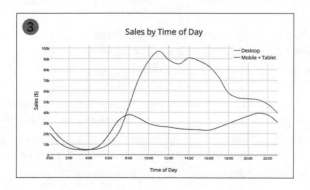

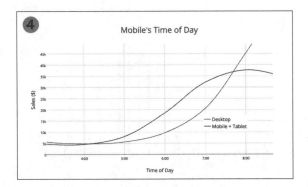

Suppose a marketing manager believes that at certain times of the day more customers shop his site on mobile devices than on desktops, but his marketing programs aren't designed to take advantage of that. He loads some data into an online tool (called Datawrapper) to see if he's right (1 on previous page).

He can't yet confirm or refute his hypothesis. He can't tell much of anything, but he's prototyping and using a tool that makes it easy to try different views into the data. He works fast; design is not a concern. He tries a line chart instead of a bar chart (2).

Now he's seeing something, but working with three variables still doesn't quite get at the mobile-versus-desktop view he wants, so he tries again with two variables (3). Each time he iterates, he evaluates whether he can confirm his original hypothesis: At certain times of day more customers are shopping on mobile devices than on desktops.

On the fourth try he zooms in and confirms his hypothesis (4).

New software tools mean this type of visualization is easier than ever before: They're making data analysts of us all.

Visual exploration. Open-ended data-driven visualizations tend to be the province of data scientists and business intelligence analysts, although new tools have begun to engage general managers in visual exploration. It's exciting to try, because it often produces insights that can't be gleaned any other way.

Because we don't know what we're looking for, these visuals tend to plot data more inclusively. In extreme cases, this kind of project may combine multiple data sets or load dynamic, real-time data into a system that updates automatically. Statistical modeling benefits from visual exploration.

Exploration also lends itself to interactivity: Managers can adjust parameters, inject new data sources, and continually revisualize. Complex data sometimes also suits specialized and unusual visualization, such as *force-directed diagrams* that show how networks cluster, or topographical plots.

Function trumps form here: Analytical, programming, data management, and business intelligence skills are more crucial than the ability to create presentable charts. Not surprisingly, this half of the quadrant is where managers are most likely to call in experts to help set up systems to wrangle data and create visualizations that fit their analytic goals.

Anmol Garg, a data scientist at Tesla Motors, has used visual exploration to tap into the vast amount of sensor data the company's cars produce. Garg created an interactive chart that shows the pressure in a car's tires over time. In true exploratory form, he and his team first created the visualizations and then found a variety of uses for them: to see whether tires are properly inflated when a car leaves the factory, how often customers reinflate them, and how long customers take to respond to a low-pressure alert; to find leak rates; and to do some predictive modeling on when tires are likely to go flat. The pressure of all four tires is visualized on a scatter plot, which, however inscrutable to a general audience, is clear to its intended audience.

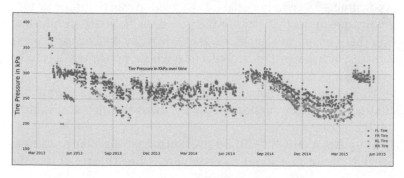

49

Garg was exploring data to find insights that could be gleaned only through visuals. "We're dealing with terabytes of data all the time," he says. "You can't find anything looking at spreadsheets and querying databases. It has to be visual." For presentations to the executive team, Garg translates these exploration sessions into the kinds of simpler charts discussed below. "Management loves seeing visualizations," he says.

Everyday dataviz

Info type	Simple, low volume
Typical setting	Formal, presentations
Primary skills	Design, storytelling
Goals	Affirming, setting context

Whereas data scientists do most of the work on visual exploration, managers do most of the work on everyday visualizations. This quadrant comprises the basic charts and graphs you normally paste from a spreadsheet into a presentation. They are usually simple—line charts, bar charts, pies, and scatter plots.

"Simple" is the key. Ideally, the visualization will communicate a single message, charting only a few variables. And the goal is straightforward: affirming and setting context. Simplicity is primarily a design challenge, so design skills are important. Clarity and consistency make these charts most effective in the setting where they're typically used: a formal presentation. In a presentation, time is constrained. A poorly designed chart will waste that time by provoking questions that require the presenter to interpret information that's meant to be obvious. If an everyday dataviz can't speak for itself, it has failed—just like a joke whose punch line has to be explained.

That's not to say that declarative charts shouldn't generate discussion. But the discussion should be about the idea in the chart, not the chart itself.

Suppose an HR VP will be presenting to the rest of the executive committee about the company's health care costs. She wants to convey that the growth of these costs has slowed significantly, creating an opportunity to invest in additional health care services.

The VP has read an online report about this trend that includes a link to some government data. She downloads the data and clicks on the line chart option in Excel. She has her viz in a few seconds. But because this is for a presentation, she asks a designer colleague to add detail from the data set to give a more comprehensive view.

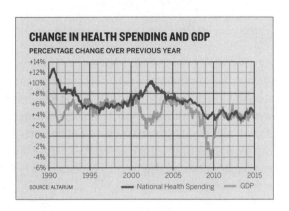

CHANGE IN HEALTH SPENDING AND GDP
PERCENTAGE CHANGE OVER PREVIOUS YEAR

This is a well-designed, accurate chart, but it's probably not the right one. The executive committee doesn't need two decades' worth of historical context to discuss the company's strategy for employee benefits investments. The point the VP wants to make is that cost increases have slowed over the past few years. Is that clearly communicated here?

In general, when it takes more than a few seconds to digest the data in a chart, the chart will work better on paper or on a personal-device screen, for someone who's not expected to listen to a presentation while trying to take in so much information. For example, health care policy makers might benefit from seeing this chart in advance of a hearing at which they'll discuss these long-term trends.

Our VP needs something cleaner for her context. She could make her point as simply as this:

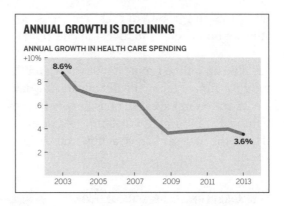

ANNUAL GROWTH IS DECLINING

ANNUAL GROWTH IN HEALTH CARE SPENDING

Simplicity like this takes some discipline—and courage—to achieve. The impulse is to include everything you know. Busy charts communicate the idea that you've been just that—busy. "Look at all the data I have and the work I've done," they seem to say. But that's not the VP's goal. She wants to persuade her colleagues to invest in new programs. With this chart, she won't have to utter a word for the executive team to understand the trend. She has clearly established a foundation for her recommendations.

In some ways, "data visualization" is a terrible term. It seems to reduce the construction of good charts to a mechanical procedure. It evokes the tools and methodology required to create rather than the creation itself. It's like calling *Moby-Dick* a "word sequentialization" or *The Starry Night* a "pigment distribution."

It also reflects an ongoing obsession in the dataviz world with process over outcomes. Visualization is merely a process. What we actually do when we make a good chart is get at some truth and move people to feel it—to see what couldn't be seen before. To change minds. To cause action.

Some basic common grammar will improve our ability to communicate visually. But good outcomes require a broader understanding and a strategic approach—which the typology described here is meant to help you develop.

Originally published June 2016. Reprint R1606H

Right Tech, Wrong Time

by Ron Adner and Rahul Kapoor

FOR THE PAST 30 YEARS, "creative destruction" has been a source of fascination at top-tier business schools and in magazines like this one. The almost obsessive interest in this topic is unsurprising, given the ever-changing, never-ending list of transformative threats—which today include the internet of things, 3-D printing, cloud computing, personalized medicine, alternative energy, and virtual reality.

Our understanding of the shifts that disrupt businesses, industries, and sectors has profoundly improved over the past 20 years: We know far more about how to identify those shifts and what dangers they pose to incumbent firms. But the *timing* of technological change remains a mystery. Even as some technologies and enterprises seem to take off overnight (ride sharing and Uber; social networking and Twitter), others take decades to unfold (high-definition TV, cloud computing). For firms and their managers, this creates a problem: Although we have become quite savvy about determining *whether* a new innovation poses a threat, we have very poor tools for knowing *when* such a transition will happen.

The number-one fear is being ready too late and missing the revolution (consider Blockbuster, which failed because it ignored the shift from video rentals to streaming). But the number-two fear should probably be getting ready too soon and exhausting resources before the revolution begins (think of any dot-com firm that died in the 2001 technology crash, only to see its ideas reborn later as a profitable Web 2.0 venture). This fear of acting prematurely applies both to established incumbents being threatened by disruptive change and to innovating start-ups carrying the flag of disruption.

To understand why some new technologies quickly supplant their predecessors while others catch on only gradually, we need to think about two things differently. First, we must look not just at the technology itself but also at the broader *ecosystem* that supports it. Second, we need to understand that competition may take place *between the new and the old ecosystems,* rather than between the technologies themselves. This perspective can help managers better predict the timing of transitions, craft more-coherent strategies for prioritizing threats and opportunities, and ultimately make wiser decisions about when and where to allocate organizational resources.

You're Only as Good as Your Ecosystem

Both established and disruptive initiatives depend on an array of complementary elements—technologies, services, standards, regulations—to deliver on their value propositions. The strength and maturity of the elements that make up the ecosystem play a key role in the success of new technologies—and the continued relevance of old ones.

The new technology's ecosystem

In assessing an emerging technology's potential, the paramount concern is whether it can satisfy customer needs and deliver value in a better way. To answer that question, investors and executives tend to drill down to specifics: How much additional development will be required before the technology is ready for commercial prime time? What will its production economics look like? Will it be price-competitive?

If the answers suggest that the new technology can really deliver on its promise, the natural expectation is that it will take over the market. Crucially, however, this expectation will hold only if the new technology's dependence on other innovations is low. For

Idea in Brief

The Problem

Over the past 20 years we've gotten very good at predicting whether a major new technology will supplant an older one—but we are still terrible at predicting when that substitution will take place.

The Insight

If the new technology doesn't need a new ecosystem to support it—if it is essentially plug-and-play— then adoption can be swift. But if other complements are needed, then the pace of substitution will

slow until those challenges are resolved. Change takes even longer when the old technology gets a boost from improvements in its own ecosystem.

The Implications

Start-ups need to consider not just when their innovation will be viable, but also what external bottlenecks will arise. Incumbents, meanwhile, should use the transition period to up their own game—and to figure out a strategy for long-term survival.

example, a new lightbulb technology that can plug into an existing socket can deliver its promised performance right out of the box. In such cases, where the value proposition does not hinge on external factors, great product execution translates into great results.

However, many technologies do not fall into this plug-and-play mold. Rather, their ability to create value depends on the development and commercial deployment of other critical parts of the ecosystem. Consider HDTV, which could not gain traction until high-definition cameras, new broadcast standards, and updated production and postproduction processes also became commercially available. Until the entire ecosystem was ready, the technology revolution promised by HDTV was bound to be delayed, no matter how great its potential for a better viewing experience. For the pioneers who developed HDTV technology in the 1980s, being right about the vision brought little comfort during the 30 years it took for the rest of the ecosystem to emerge.

An improved lightbulb and an HDTV both depend on ecosystems of complementary elements. The difference is that the lightbulb plugs into an existing ecosystem (established power generation and distribution networks; wired homes), whereas the television requires the successful development of co-innovations. Improvements in the lightbulb will thus create immediate value for customers, but the TV's ability to create value is limited by the availability and progress of other elements in its ecosystem.

The old technology's ecosystem

Successful, established technologies—by definition—have overcome their emergence challenges and are embedded within successful, established ecosystems. Whereas new technologies can be held back by their ecosystems, incumbent technologies can be accelerated by improvements in theirs, even in the absence of progress in the core technology itself. For example, although the basic technology behind bar codes has not changed in decades, their utility improves every year as the IT infrastructure supporting them allows ever-more information to be extracted. Hence in the 1980s, bar codes allowed prices to be automatically scanned into cash registers; in the 1990s, aggregating the bar code data from daily or weekly transactions provided insight into general inventory; in the modern era, bar code data is used for real-time inventory management and supply chain restocking. Similarly, improvements in DSL (digital subscriber line) technology have extended the life of copper telephone lines, which can now offer download speeds of 15 megabytes per second, making copper-wire services competitive with newer cable and fiber networks.

The War Between Ecosystems

When a new technology isn't a simple plug-and-play substitution—when it requires significant developments in the ecosystem in order to be useful—then a race between the new- and the old-technology ecosystems begins.

What determines who wins? For the *new* technology, the key factor is how quickly its ecosystem becomes sufficiently developed for users to realize the technology's potential. In the case of cloud-based applications and storage, for example, success depended not just on figuring out how to manage data in server farms, but also on

About the Research

WE DEVELOPED AND EXPLORED the ideas described in this article during a five-year research project on the pace of substitution in the semiconductor-manufacturing ecosystem.

The semiconductor industry's remarkably robust progress over the past 60 years was made possible by innovations in the lithography technology that semiconductor manufacturers use. We studied the successive generations of lithography equipment and noticed a pattern: In some cases, the new technology dominated the market in a matter of two to five years, whereas in other cases it faced prolonged, unexpected delays in achieving market dominance—and sometimes never did. This was true despite the fact that each generation offered superior performance, even on a price-adjusted performance basis.

To test our hypotheses about how ecosystem emergence challenges and extension opportunities affect the pace of substitution, we first collected and analyzed detailed data on every product and firm involved in every generation of the technology. We supplemented that information with extensive interviews with executives from firms throughout the ecosystem.

Our statistical analysis showed that 48% of the variation in the pace of substitution was attributable to traditional factors: price-adjusted performance differences, the number of rivals in the market, and the tenure of the old technology. When we added consideration of the ecosystem dynamics discussed in the article, we were able to account for a remarkable 82% of the variance.

For more details on the research, see "Innovation Ecosystems and the Pace of Substitution: Re-examining Technology S-Curves," by Ron Adner and Rahul Kapoor, *Strategic Management Journal* (March 2015).

ensuring the satisfactory performance of critical complements such as broadband and online security. For the *old* technology, what's important is how its competitiveness can be increased by improvement in the established ecosystem. In the case of desktop storage systems (the technology that cloud-based applications would replace), extension opportunities have historically included faster interfaces and more-robust components. As these opportunities become exhausted, we can expect substitution to accelerate.

Thus the pace of substitution is determined by the rate at which the new technology's ecosystem can overcome its emergence challenges relative to the rate at which the old technology's ecosystem can exploit its extension opportunities. To consider the interplay between these forces, we have developed a framework to help managers assess how quickly disruptive change is coming to their industry (see the chart "A framework for analyzing the pace of technology substitution"). There are four possible scenarios: creative destruction, robust resilience, robust coexistence, and the illusion of resilience.

Creative destruction

When the ecosystem emergence challenge for the new technology is low and the ecosystem extension opportunity for the old technology is also low (quadrant 1 in the framework), the new technology can be expected to achieve market dominance in short order (see point A in the exhibit "How fast does new technology replace the old?"). The new technology's ability to create value is not held back by bottlenecks elsewhere in the ecosystem, and the old technology has limited potential to improve in response to the threat. This quadrant aligns with concept of creative destruction—the idea that an innovative upstart can swiftly cause the demise of established competitors. While the old technology can continue serving niches for a long time (see "Bold Retreat," by Ron Adner and Daniel C. Snow, HBR, March 2010), the bulk of the market will abandon it relatively quickly in favor of the new technology. As an example, consider the rapid replacement of dot matrix printers by inkjet printers.

Robust resilience

When the balance is reversed—when the new technology's ecosystem confronts serious emergence challenges and the old technology's ecosystem has strong opportunities to improve (quadrant 4)—the pace of substitution will be very slow. The old technology can be expected to maintain a prosperous leadership position for an extended period. This quadrant is most consistent with technologies that seem revolutionary when they're first touted but appear overhyped in retrospect.

Bar codes and radio frequency identification (RFID) chips provide a good example. RFID chips hold the promise of storing far richer

A framework for analyzing the pace of technology substitution

The pace of substitution is determined by how quickly the new technology's ecosystem challenges are resolved and whether the old technology can exploit ecosystem opportunities for extension.

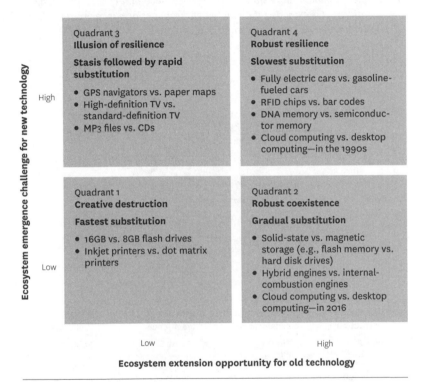

Quadrant 3
Illusion of resilience

Stasis followed by rapid substitution

- GPS navigators vs. paper maps
- High-definition TV vs. standard-definition TV
- MP3 files vs. CDs

Quadrant 4
Robust resilience

Slowest substitution

- Fully electric cars vs. gasoline-fueled cars
- RFID chips vs. bar codes
- DNA memory vs. semiconductor memory
- Cloud computing vs. desktop computing—in the 1990s

Quadrant 1
Creative destruction

Fastest substitution

- 16GB vs. 8GB flash drives
- Inkjet printers vs. dot matrix printers

Quadrant 2
Robust coexistence

Gradual substitution

- Solid-state vs. magnetic storage (e.g., flash memory vs. hard disk drives)
- Hybrid engines vs. internal-combustion engines
- Cloud computing vs. desktop computing—in 2016

High

Low

Ecosystem emergence challenge for new technology

Low   High

Ecosystem extension opportunity for old technology

data than bar codes ever could, but their adoption has lagged because of the slow deployment of suitable IT infrastructure and non-uniform industry standards. Meanwhile, IT improvements have extended the usability of bar code data, as we've already discussed, relegating RFID to niche applications and keeping the RFID revolution at bay for the past two decades. It may well be that RFID does eventually overcome its challenges and that ecosystem extension opportunities dry up for bar codes. If this happens, the dynamics

How fast does new technology replace the old?

Traditionally the substitution of a new technology for an old one is shown with two S curves (the solid lines). A more holistic view adds two more dynamics. First, if the new technology depends on the emergence of a new ecosystem, it becomes dominant more slowly (dotted line). Second, the old technology's competitiveness is extended if it can benefit from performance improvements in its surrounding ecosystem (dashed line).

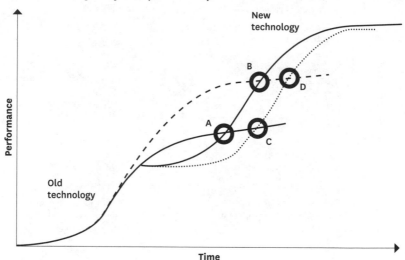

Creative destruction	Robust coexistence	Illusion of resilience	Robust resilience
Point A The classic—and fastest—substitution takes place when the new technology's ecosystem is ready to go and the old technology's ecosystem can't be significantly improved.	**Point B** If the new technology is compatible with the existing ecosystem and the old technology's ecosystem can be significantly improved, substitution takes place later (relative to creative destruction) and at a higher performance level.	**Point C** If the new technology's ecosystem needs considerable development and the old technology's ecosystem has little room for improvement, the changeover occurs after time has passed without performance gains.	**Point D** If the new technology's ecosystem needs considerable development and there are abundant opportunities to improve the old technology's ecosystem, the substitution occurs after the longest period of time and at the highest performance level.

Note: The exact positions of B and C will depend on the specifics of the case, but they will reflect an intermediate pace of substitution (relative to points A and D) and intermediate performance at substitution.

will shift from quadrant 4 to another quadrant, and the pace of substitution will quicken. But that will be small consolation to the firms and investors that committed to RFID decades ago. The opportunity cost of waiting for the rest of the system to catch up can mean that being in the right place 10 years too soon is more costly than missing the revolution completely.

When substitution is slow, there are also implications for the new technology's required performance levels (see point D in the exhibit). Every time IT improvements make bar codes more useful, for example, the quality threshold for the RFID technology is raised. Thus performance expectations for the innovation keep ratcheting upward, even as its wide adoption is held back by the underdeveloped state of its ecosystem.

Robust coexistence
When the ecosystem emergence challenge for the new technology is low and the ecosystem extension opportunity for the old technology is high (quadrant 2), competition will be robust. The new technology will make inroads into the market, but improvements in the old-technology ecosystem will allow the incumbent to defend its market share. There will be a prolonged period of coexistence. Although extension opportunities are unlikely to reverse the rise of the new technology, they will materially delay its dominance.

An instructive example is the competition between hybrid (gas-electric) automobile engines and traditional internal-combustion engines. Unlike fully electric engines, which need a supporting network of charging stations, hybrids were not held back by ecosystem emergence challenges. At the same time, however, traditional gas engines have become more fuel-efficient, and the ecosystem for the traditional technology has improved, too, as gas engines have become better integrated with other elements in the vehicle, such as heating and cooling systems.

A period of robust coexistence can be quite attractive from a consumer perspective. Performance of both ecosystems is improving—and the better the old technology's ecosystem becomes, the higher the performance bar is for the new technology's ecosystem (point B in the exhibit).

The illusion of resilience

When the ecosystem emergence challenge is high for the new technology and the ecosystem extension opportunity is low for the old technology (quadrant 3), not much will change until the emergence challenge is resolved—but then substitution will be rapid (point C in the exhibit). Examples here are HDTVs versus traditional TVs, and e-books versus printed books. Both of those revolutions were delayed not by advances in the old technology's ecosystem but by ecosystem-emergence challenges in the new technology.

In scenarios in this quadrant, an industry analysis will most likely show that the old technology maintains high market share, but growth has stalled. Because rapid market-share inversion is to be expected once the new technology fulfills its value creation potential, the dominance of the old technology is fragile. It is maintained not by continued progress in the old technology but by setbacks for the new competitor.

Implications for Action

Once you understand that in the race to dominance, ecosystems are just as important as technologies, you will be better at thinking through how quickly change is going to occur—and deciding what level of performance you need to aim for in the meantime. We will consider how to tackle these questions shortly, but first let's review a few general truths that emerge from this perspective.

- If your company is introducing a potentially transformative innovation, the full value will not be realized until all bottlenecks in the ecosystem are resolved. It may pay to focus a little less on perfecting the technology itself and a little more on resolving the most pressing problems in the ecosystem.

- If you are a threatened incumbent, it pays to analyze not just the emerging technology itself but also the ecosystem that supports it. The greater the ecosystem-emergence challenge for the new technology, the more time you have to strengthen your own performance.

- Strengthening incumbent performance may mean improving the old technology—but it can just as easily mean improving aspects of the ecosystem that supports it.

- Every time the old technology's performance gets better, the performance threshold for the new technology goes up.

With that overview in mind, let's look at how to use this framework to analyze your own technology strategy. We recommend having executive conversations focused on two questions: Which quadrant is our industry in? and What are the implications for our resource allocation and other strategic choices?

Which quadrant are we in?

Without the benefit of hindsight, your response to this question is clearly a matter of judgment. Some people would look at electric vehicles in 2016 and say they are still stuck in quadrant 4 (where we have placed them in our framework), pointing out that the charging infrastructure and battery performance are insufficient for mainstream adoption. Other people would position EVs on the cusp of quadrant 2, claiming that acceptance is growing and that better batteries make it possible to drive longer distances before recharging. Still others would place EVs solidly in quadrant 2, arguing that Tesla's success in selling its vehicles and populating its waiting lists is a sure sign that commercial potential is no longer constrained.

The sidebar "How Big a Threat Is the New Technology?" suggests issues to think through as you debate which quadrant you're in. Some questions pertain to the new technology and some to the old—but you will want to consider them all, regardless of whether you are an incumbent or a start-up. Don't expect all individual team members to agree on the answers to these questions. It is precisely by going through the process of articulating different views that teams can make the most of their collective insights.

How Big a Threat Is the New Technology?

PREDICTING THE PACE OF SUBSTITUTION requires analyzing the competition between the new- and the old-technology ecosystems. Six questions can help innovators and incumbents assess their positions and strategies.

New-Technology Questions

These questions (drawn from *The Wide Lens,* by coauthor Ron Adner) address the emergence challenges that confront the new technology. The answers should help innovators decide how to adjust their strategies.

1. What is the *execution risk*—the level of difficulty in delivering the focal innovation to the market on time and to spec?

2. What is the *co-innovation risk*—the extent to which the success of the new technology depends on the successful commercialization of other innovations?

3. What is the *adoption-chain risk*—the extent to which other partners need to adopt and adapt to the new technology before end consumers can fully assess its value proposition?

The greater the extent to which the new technology is facing any of these risks, the greater the challenge to be overcome, and the longer the expected delay in adoption of the technology.

Old-Technology Questions

These questions address the prospects for improving the competitiveness of the incumbent technology. The answers should help incumbents identify opportunities they might exploit.

1. Can the competitiveness of the old technology be extended by further improvements to the technology itself?

2. Can it be extended by improvements to complementary elements in its ecosystem?

3. Can it be extended by borrowing from innovations in the new technology and its ecosystem?

The more positive the reply to each of these questions, the greater the extension opportunity for the old technology.

What are the implications for resource allocation and other strategic choices?

Each quadrant in the framework carries different implications for resource allocation decisions. And since markets are not transformed all at once, the quadrant also suggests possible ways to position yourself during the transition.

In quadrant 1 (creative destruction), with the old technology stagnant and the new technology unhampered, innovators should aggressively invest in the new technology. Incumbents should follow the familiar prescriptions for embracing change to withstand the winds of creative destruction. Part of that is looking for niche positions where they can survive in the long term with the old technology. For example, pagers were largely replaced by cell phones, but they are still used by emergency-service providers.

In quadrant 2 (robust coexistence), incumbent firms can continue to invest in the old technology and aggressively invest in improvements to the ecosystem, knowing that the new and the old technologies will coexist for an extended period. As in quadrant 1, they should also seek niche positions for the old technology for the long term, but there is less urgency to do so. New-technology innovators should move full speed ahead on perfecting the new technology along with its complements. That includes testing and refining the offering with early adopters and segments that are potentially receptive.

In quadrant 3 (the illusion of resilience), new-technology champions should direct resources toward resolving their ecosystem challenges and developing complementary elements, and resist overprioritizing further development of the technology itself. When the bottleneck to adoption is the ecosystem, not the technology, pushing technology progress is pushing the wrong lever. Incumbents, for their part, must guard against the false assumption that they are maintaining their market position because of the merits of their own technology. As publishers of road atlases will attest, this is probably a time to harvest and make only incremental improvements, with an eye toward sunset; it is not the time to redouble innovation efforts in the old technology.

Finally, in quadrant 4 (robust resilience), incumbent firms should invest aggressively in upgrading their offerings and actively raising the bar that challengers need to cross. Obviously, new-technology innovators should be clear-eyed about working to resolve the ecosystem constraints they face. But at the same time they must recognize that the performance threshold for their core technology is rising. That necessitates both a significant level of resource investment and considerable patience regarding investment returns. Innovators are not likely to transform the sector in the foreseeable future, and therefore they will want to think through the economics of serving those customers they can succeed with.

One final note about the dynamics of change. Every innovator wants to end up in quadrant 1 so that it can play the classic creative-destruction game. But there are different paths for getting there. A hypothesis that predicts a transition path from Q4 to Q3 to Q1 is a bet on the exhaustion of the old technology. For an innovator, that would mean focusing on aligning the new-technology ecosystem without great concern for extending a performance advantage. In contrast, a predicted path of Q4 to Q2 to Q1 would mean competing against an improving incumbent-technology ecosystem. Here the innovator needs to continually elevate its performance while it simultaneously perfects the ecosystem.

Few modern firms are untouched by the urgency of innovation. But when it comes to strategizing for a revolution, the question of "whether" often drowns out the question of "when." Unfortunately, getting the first right but not the second can be devastating. "Right tech, wrong time" syndrome is a nightmare for any innovating firm. Closer analysis of the enabling contexts of rival technologies—Is the new ecosystem ready to roll? Does the old ecosystem still hold potential for improvement?—sheds more light on the question of timing. And better timing, in turn, will improve the efficiency and effectiveness of the innovation efforts that are so critical for survival and success.

Further Reading

FOR MORE INSIGHTS INTO THE relationship between technologies and their ecosystems, see the following:

- **"Match Your Innovation Strategy to Your Innovation Ecosystem,"** Ron Adner, HBR, April 2006

- **"A Sad Lesson in Collaborative Innovation,"** Ron Adner, HBR.org, May 9, 2012

- *The Wide Lens: What Successful Innovators See That Others Miss,* Ron Adner, Portfolio/Penguin 2013

- **"Beware of Old Technologies' Last Gasps,"** Daniel Snow, HBR, January 2008

- **"Value Creation in Innovation Ecosystems: How the Structure of Technological Interdependence Affects Firm Performance in New Technology Generations,"** Ron Adner and Rahul Kapoor, *Strategic Management Journal* March 2010

Originally published in November 2016. Reprint R1611C

How to Pay for Health Care

by Michael E. Porter and Robert S. Kaplan

THE UNITED STATES STANDS at a crossroads as it struggles with how to pay for health care. The fee-for-service system, the dominant payment model in the U.S. and many other countries, is now widely recognized as perhaps the single biggest obstacle to improving health care delivery.

Fee for service rewards the quantity but not the quality or efficiency of medical care. The most common alternative payment system today—fixed annual budgets for providers—is not much better, since the budgets are disconnected from the actual patient needs that arise during the year. Fixed budgets inevitably lead to long waits for nonemergency care and create pressure to increase budgets each year.

We need a better way to pay for health care, one that rewards providers for delivering superior value to patients: that is, for achieving better health outcomes at lower cost. The move toward "value-based reimbursement" is accelerating, which is an encouraging trend. And the Centers for Medicare & Medicaid Services (CMS), to its credit, is leading the charge in the United States.

That doesn't mean, however, that health care is converging on a solution. The broad phrase "value-based reimbursement" encompasses two radically different payment approaches: capitation and bundled payments. In capitation, the health care organization receives a fixed payment per year per covered life and must meet all the needs of a broad patient population. In a bundled payment system, by contrast, providers are paid for the care of a patient's medical condition across the entire care cycle—that is, all the services, procedures, tests, drugs, and devices used to treat a patient with, say, heart failure, an arthritic hip that needs replacement, or diabetes. If this sounds familiar, it's because it is the way we usually pay for other products and services we purchase.

A battle is raging, largely unbeknownst to the general public, between advocates of these two approaches. The stakes are high, and the outcome will define the shape of the health care system for many years to come, for better or for worse. While we recognize that capitation can achieve modest savings in the short run, we believe that it is not the right solution. It threatens patient choice and competition and will fail to fundamentally change the trajectory of a broken system. A bundled payment system, however, would truly transform the way we deliver care and finally put health care on the right path.

The Small Step: Capitation

Capitation, or population-based payment, is not a new idea. It was introduced in the United States with some fanfare in the 1990s but quickly ran into widespread criticism and was scaled back significantly. Today, a number of transitional approaches, including accountable care organizations (ACOs), shared savings plans, and alternative quality contracts, have been introduced as steps toward capitation. In the ACO model, the care organization earns bonuses or penalties on the basis of how the total fee-for-service charges for all the population's treatments during the year compare with historical charges. In full capitation, the care organization absorbs the difference between the sum of capitation payments and its actual cost.

Under capitation, unlike in the FFS model, the payer (insurer) no longer reimburses various providers for each service delivered. Rather, it makes a single payment for each subscriber (usually per patient per month) to a single delivery organization. The approach

Idea in Brief

The Challenge

The United States stands at a crossroads as it struggles with how to pay for health care. Fee for service, the dominant model today, is widely recognized as the single biggest obstacle to improving health care delivery. The choice is between two fundamentally different approaches: capitation and bundled payments. The stakes are high, and the outcome will define the shape of the health care system for many years to come, for better or for worse.

The Danger

Although capitation may deliver modest savings in the short run, it is not the solution. It entrenches large existing systems, eliminates patient choice, promotes consolidation, limits competition, and perpetuates the lack of accountability for outcomes. Like fee for service, capitation will fail to drive true innovation in health care delivery.

The Opportunity

Bundled payments trigger competition among providers to create value where it matters—at the individual patient level—and will finally put health care on the right path. Robust proof-of-concept initiatives in the U.S. and abroad demonstrate that the challenges of transitioning to bundled payments are already being overcome.

rewards providers for lowering the overall cost of treating the population, which is a step forward. However, under this system cost reduction gravitates toward population-level approaches targeting generic high-cost areas, such as limiting the use of expensive tests and drugs, reducing readmissions, shortening lengths of stay, and discharging patients to their homes rather than to higher-cost rehabilitation facilities. As a response to the failed experience with capitation in the 1990s, current capitation approaches include some provider accountability for quality. However, "quality" is measured by broad population-level metrics, such as patient satisfaction, process compliance, and overall outcomes such as complication and readmission rates.

This all seems good at first blush. The trouble is that, like the failed FFS payment system, capitation creates competition at the wrong level and on the wrong things, rather than on what really matters to patients and to the health care system overall.

Providers are not accountable for patient-level value

Capitation and its variants reward improvement at the population level, but patients don't care about population outcomes such as overall infection rates; they care about the treatments they receive to address their particular needs. Outcomes that matter to breast cancer patients are different from those that are important to patients with heart failure. Even for primary and preventive care, which the concept of population health rightly emphasizes, appropriate care depends heavily on each patient's circumstances—health status, comorbidities, disability, and so on. And managing the overall health of a diverse population with high turnover (as ACOs do) is extremely difficult.

Thus, capitated payments are not aligned with better or efficient care for each patient's particular condition. Instead, capitation puts the focus on limiting the overall amount of care delivered without tying the outcomes back to individual patients or providers. The wrong incentives are created, just as is the case for fee for service, which reimburses for the volume of services but not the value.

Providers bear the wrong risks

Because capitation pays providers a fee per person covered, it shifts the risk for the cost of the population's actual mix of medical needs—over which they have only limited control—to providers. Some large private insurers favor capitation for just this reason. But bearing the actuarial risk of a population's medical needs is what insurers should do, since they cover a far larger and more diverse patient population over which to spread this risk. Providers should bear only the risks related to the actual care they deliver, which they can directly affect.

A more fundamental problem is that capitation payments are extremely difficult to adjust to reflect each patient's overall health risk, not to mention to correctly adjust for this risk across a large, diverse population. Risks are much better understood and managed for a particular medical condition—for example, the probable effects of age or comorbidities on the costs and outcomes for joint replacement—as is the case in bundled payments.

Because population-level risk factors are so complex, health systems under capitation have an incentive to claim as many comorbidities as possible to bolster their revenue and profitability. A whole segment of health care IT providers has emerged to help providers "upcode" patients into higher-risk categories. Such gaming of risk adjustment first became a problem during the era of managed-care capitation in the 1990s, and it remains one today.

Patient choice is limited, and competition is threatened
Capitation creates strong incentives for a health system to deliver all the care within its system, because contracting for outside services reduces net revenue and results in underutilization of existing internal capacity. There is even a term for this in health care—"avoiding leakage"—and many systems explicitly monitor and control it. Capitated health systems encourage or require patients (and their referring doctors) to use in-house providers (the ultimate narrow network). Patients are often penalized with extra fees when they don't use services within the system, even if outside providers have greater experience and get better results for treating the patient's particular condition. Capitation creates, in essence, a monopoly provider for all the patients in the population. Consumers cannot choose the best provider for their particular needs.

Since providers now bear actuarial risk, they also have a strong incentive to amass the largest possible population. This will accelerate the recent trend of providers' buying up other hospitals and physician practices and merging systems, which reduces competition. To offset health systems' rising bargaining power, insurers will feel pressure to merge. The two dynamics will reinforce each other as provider consolidation begets even more insurer consolidation.

The end result will be the emergence of a few dominant systems—or even only one—in each region. This would be bad for patients. No one organization can have all the skills and technologies needed to be the best in treating everything. We need multiple providers in each region to ensure enough choice and drive innovation in care delivery.

The bottom line is that capitation is the wrong way to pay for health care. It is a top-down approach that achieves some cost savings by targeting low-hanging fruit such as readmission rates, expensive drugs, and better management of post-acute care. But it does not really change health care delivery, nor does it hold providers accountable for efficiency and outcomes where they matter to patients—in the treatment of their particular condition. Capitation's savings also come at the high cost of restricting patient choice and inhibiting provider competition.

Let's consider the alternative.

Paying for Value: Bundled Payments

For virtually all types of products and services, customers pay a single price for the whole package that meets their needs. When purchasing a car, for example, consumers don't buy the motor from one supplier, the brakes from another, and so on; they buy the complete product from a single entity. It makes just as little sense for patients to buy their diagnostic tests from one provider, surgical services from another, and post-acute care from yet another. Bundled payments may sound complicated, but in setting a single price for all the care required to treat a patient's particular medical condition, they actually draw on the approach long used in virtually every other industry.

Bundled payments have existed in health care for some time in isolated fields such as organ transplantation. They are also common for services that patients pay for directly, such as Lasik eye surgery, plastic surgery, and in vitro fertilization.

To maximize value for the patient, a bundled payment must meet five conditions:

Payment covers the overall care required to treat a condition
The bundled payment should cover the full cost of treating a patient over the entire care cycle for a given condition or over time for chronic conditions or primary care. The scope of care should be defined from the patient's perspective ("Delivering a healthy

child"). Care should include all needed services, including managing common comorbidities and related complications. In primary and preventive care, bundled payments should include all the needed care for each defined patient segment (such as healthy adults or low-income elderly).

Payment is contingent on delivering good outcomes
Bundled payments should be tied to achieving the outcomes that matter to patients for each condition and primary care patient segment. Important outcomes include maintaining or returning to normal function, reducing pain, and avoiding and reducing complications or recurrences.

Payment is adjusted for risk
Differences in patients' age and health status affect the complexity, outcomes, and cost of treating a particular condition, as do their social and living circumstances. These risk factors should be reflected in the bundled payment and in expectations for outcomes to reward providers for taking on hard cases.

Payment provides a fair profit for effective and efficient care
A bundled payment should cover the full costs of the necessary care, plus a margin, for providers that use effective and efficient clinical and administrative processes. It should not cover unnecessary services or inefficient care.

Providers are not responsible for unrelated care or catastrophic cases
Providers should be responsible only for care related to the condition—not for care such as emergency treatment after an accident or an unrelated cardiac event. The limits of provider responsibility should be specified in advance and subject to adjudication if disputes arise. Bundled payments should also include a "stop loss" provision to limit providers' exposure to unusually high costs from catastrophic or outlier cases. This reduces the need for providers to build such costs into the price for every patient (unlike in capitation).

How Bundled Payments Will Transform Patient Care

Decades of incremental efforts to cut costs in health care and impose practice guidelines on clinicians have failed. Bundled payments directly reward providers for delivering better value for the patient's condition and will unlock the restructuring of health care delivery in three crucial ways that capitation cannot.

Integrated, multidisciplinary care

Specialty silos have historically led to fragmented, uncoordinated, and inefficient care. With bundled payments, providers with overall responsibility for the full care cycle for a condition will be empowered and motivated to coordinate and integrate all the specialists and facilities involved in care. Clinical teams (the experts) have the freedom to decide how to spend the fixed bundled payment, rather than being required to deliver the services that are reimbursed by legacy FFS payments in order to receive revenue. Teams can choose to add services that are not currently covered by FFS but that provide value for patients.

Bundled payments are triggering a whole new level of care innovation. For example, hospital-based physicians are remaining involved in care after patients are discharged. Hospitalists are added to teams to coordinate all the inpatient specialists involved in the care cycle. Nurses make sure patients fill their prescriptions, take medications correctly, and actually see their primary care physician. (A recent study showed that 50% of readmitted patients did not see their primary care doctor in the first 30 days after discharge.) And navigators accompany patients through all phases of their care and act as first responders in quickly resolving problems. Bundled payments are also spurring innovation in the creation of tailored facilities, such as those of Twin Cities Orthopedics (Minneapolis), which performs joint-replacement care in outpatient surgery centers and nearby recovery centers, rather than in a traditional hospital.

Bundled payments will accelerate the formation of integrated practice units (IPUs), such as MD Anderson's Head and Neck Center and the Joslin Diabetes Center. IPUs combine all the relevant clinicians and support personnel in one team, working in dedicated

How Fee for Service Destroys Value for Patients

FEE-FOR-SERVICE REIMBURSEMENT, the dominant method used to pay for health care in the United States and elsewhere, has held back improvements in the quality of care and led to escalating costs. Overturning the status quo is not easy, but here's why doing so is essential.

Rewards poor outcomes

Because FFS reimburses providers on the basis of volume of care, providers are rewarded not just for performing unnecessary services but for poor outcomes. Complications, revisions, and recurrences all result in the need for additional services, for which providers get reimbursed again.

Fosters duplication and lack of coordination

FFS makes payments for individual procedures and services, rather than for the treatment of a patient's condition over the entire care cycle. In response, providers have organized around functional specialties (such as radiology). Today, multiple independent providers are involved in each patient's treatment, resulting in poorly coordinated care, duplicated services, and no accountability for health outcomes.

Perpetuates inefficiency

Today's FFS payments reflect historical reimbursements with arbitrary inflation adjustments, not true costs. Reimbursement levels vary widely, causing cross-subsidization across specialties and particular services. The misalignment means that inefficient providers can survive, and even thrive, despite high costs and poor outcomes.

Reduces focus

FFS motivates providers to offer full services for all types of conditions to grow overall revenue, even as internal fragmentation causes patients to be handed off from one specialty to another. By attempting to cater to a diverse population of patients, providers fail to develop the specialized capabilities and experience in any one condition necessary for the delivery of excellent care.

---

facilities. Joslin, for example, brings together all the specialists (endocrinologists, nephrologists, internists, neurologists, ophthalmologists, and psychiatrists) and all the support personnel (nurses, educators, dieticians, and exercise physiologists) required to provide high-value diabetes care. IPUs concentrate volume of patients with a given condition in one place, allowing diagnosis and treatment by a highly experienced team. Numerous studies show that this approach leads to better outcomes and greater efficiency (including less wait time and fewer visits). Bundled payments also encourage the formation of "virtual" IPUs, where even separate practices and organizations actively collaborate across inpatient and outpatient settings to coordinate and integrate care—something that rarely happens today.

Accountability for outcomes

By definition, a bundled payment holds the entire provider team accountable for achieving the outcomes that matter to patients for their condition—unlike capitation, which involves only loose accountability for patient satisfaction or population-level quality targets.

Because bundled payments are adjusted for risk, providers are rewarded for taking on difficult cases. With a fixed single payment, they are penalized if they overtreat patients or perform care in unnecessarily high-cost locations. And because providers are accountable for outcomes covering the entire care cycle, they will move quickly to add new services, more-expensive interventions, or better diagnostic tests if those will improve outcomes or lower the overall cost of care. Specialists operating under a bundled payment, for example, have added primary care physicians to their care teams to better manage the overall care cycle and deal with comorbidities.

Most important, the accountability built into bundled payments will finally bring to health care the systematic measurement of outcomes at the condition level, where it matters most. We know from every other field that measuring and being accountable for results is the most powerful driver of innovation and continuous improvement.

Cost reduction

There have been repeated efforts to control health costs for decades without success, and top-down cost reduction initiatives have sometimes increased costs rather than reduced them. The core problem is that legacy payment models such as FFS have given providers no incentive to cut costs or even to understand what their costs are for treating a given condition. Bundled payments, by contrast, directly reward and motivate cost reduction from the bottom up, team by team. At the same time, they encourage accurate cost measurement not only to inform price setting but to enable true cost reduction.

Bundled payments will be the catalyst that finally motivates provider teams to work together to understand the actual costs of each step in the entire care process, learn how to do things better, and get care right the first time. By encouraging competition for the treatment of individual conditions on the basis of quality and price, bundled payments also reward providers for standardizing care pathways, eliminating services and therapies that fail to improve outcomes, better utilizing staff to the top of their skills, and providing care in the right facilities. If providers use ineffective or unnecessary therapies or services, they will bear the cost, making bundled payments a check against overtreatment.

The result will be not just a downward "bend" in the cost curve—that is, a slower increase—but actual cost reduction. Our research suggests that savings of 20% to 30% are feasible in many conditions. And, because bundled payments are contingent on good outcomes, the right kind of cost reduction will take place, not cost cutting at the expense of quality.

Overcoming the Transition Challenges

Despite the now proven benefits of well-designed bundled payments, many hospital systems, group purchasing organizations, private insurers, and some academics prefer capitation. Bundled payments, they argue, are too complicated to design, negotiate, and implement. (They ignore the fact that capitation models continue to rely on complex, expensive fee-for-service billing to pay clinicians and to set the baseline for calculating savings and penalties. Bundled payments are actually simpler to administer than the myriad of FFS payments for each patient over the care cycle.)

Skeptics raise a host of other objections: The scope of a condition and care cycle is hard to define; it is unrealistic to expect specialists to work together; the data on outcomes and costs needed to set prices are difficult to obtain; differences in risk across patients are

A History of Success

BUNDLED PAYMENTS ARE NOT A NEW IDEA or a passing fad. Successful pilots date back for decades and include initiatives spearheaded by the Centers for Medicare & Medicaid Services.

Consider the Heart Bypass Demonstration, an initiative that ran from 1991 to 1996. CMS offered a bundled payment for coronary artery bypass graft surgery that covered all services delivered in the hospital, along with 90 days of post-discharge services. The pilot yielded savings to Medicare of $42.3 million, or roughly 10% of expected spending, at the seven participating hospitals. The inpatient mortality rate declined at all the hospitals, and patient satisfaction improved.

CMS also implemented the Acute Care Episode program (from 2009 to 2011), in which Medicare paid five participating organizations a flat fee to cover hospital and physician services for various cardiac conditions and orthopedic care. Over a total of 12,501 episodes, the initiative generated an average savings to Medicare of 3.1% of expected costs.

---

hard to assess, which will lead to cherry-picking; and bundled payments won't rein in overtreatment.

If these objections represented serious barriers, we would expect to see little progress in implementing bundled payments and plenty of evidence that such programs were unsuccessful. To the contrary, bundled payments have a history of good results (see the sidebar "A History of Success") and are currently proliferating rapidly in a wide range of conditions, organizations, and countries.

In 2007, for example, the Netherlands introduced a successful bundled payment model for treating patients with type 2 diabetes, and, later, for chronic obstructive pulmonary disease (COPD). In 2009, the County of Stockholm, Sweden, introduced bundled payments for hip and knee replacements in healthy patients, achieving a 17% reduction in cost and a 33% reduction in complications over two years. More recently, Stockholm introduced bundled payments for all major spine diagnoses requiring surgery, and extensions to other conditions are under way there.

In 2011, Medicare introduced the voluntary Bundled Payments for Care Improvement (BPCI) program, which currently includes more than 14,000 bundles in 24 medical and 24 surgical conditions.

Numerous physician practices have embraced the BPCI model, a transitional bundled payment approach that covers acute-care episodes and often a post-acute period of up to 90 days to promote better management of post-discharge services. According to participating providers, BPCI bundles have achieved significant improvements and savings an order of magnitude greater than savings from ACOs. Building on that success, CMS launched a mandatory bundled payment program for joint replacements in 2016, which covers 800 hospitals in 67 U.S. metropolitan areas.

Bundled payment contracts involving private insurers are also finally beginning to proliferate. For example, Twin Cities Orthopedics offers a bundle for joint replacement with most of the region's major insurers at a price well below the traditional hospital models. The practice reports better outcomes and cost reductions of more than 30%.

To be sure, many existing bundled payment programs have yet to encompass all the components of an ideal structure. Most have made pragmatic compromises, such as covering only part of the care cycle, using important but incomplete risk adjustments, and incorporating limited outcome measures. But even these less-than-comprehensive efforts are resulting in major improvements, and the obstacles to bundled payments are being overcome.

Let's consider some of the main criticisms of bundled payments in more depth:

Only some conditions can be covered
Critics have suggested that bundled payments apply only to elective surgical care and other well-defined acute conditions, and not to nonsurgical conditions, chronic disease, or primary care. But this claim is inconsistent with actual experience. Of the 48 conditions designated for BPCI, only half were surgical. The other half were for care episodes in nonsurgical conditions, such as heart disease, kidney disease, diabetes, and COPD. Time-based bundled payments for chronic care are emerging in other countries and with private payers. Bundled payments work well for chronic conditions because of the huge benefits that result from coordinated longitudinal care by a multidisciplinary team.

Bundled payment models are also beginning to emerge for primary and preventive care for well-defined segments of patients with similar needs. Each primary care segment—such as healthy children, healthy adults, adults at risk for developing chronic disease, and the elderly—will need a very different mix of clinical, educational, and administrative services, and the appropriate outcomes will differ as well. Bundled payments reward integrated and efficient delivery of the right mix of primary and preventive services for each patient group.

Primary care bundles need not cover the cost of treating complex, acute conditions, which are best paid for with bundled payments to IPUs covering those conditions. Instead, primary care teams should be held accountable for their performance in primary care and prevention for each patient segment: maintaining health status, avoiding disease progression, and preventing relapses.

Defining and implementing bundled payments is too complicated
Critics argue that it will be hard to negotiate bundled payments across all conditions and to get agreement on the definition of a medical condition, the extent of the care cycle, and the included services. This objection is weak at best. A manageable number of conditions account for a large proportion of health care costs, and we can start there and expand over time. The care required for most medical conditions is well established, and experience in defining bundles is rapidly accumulating. Methodologies and commercial tools, such as the use of comprehensive claims data sets, are in widespread use. Service companies that help providers define conditions, form teams, and manage payments are emerging, as are software tools that handle billing and claims processing for bundles.

Initially, bundled payments may cover less than the full care cycle, focus on simpler patient groups with a given condition, and require adjudication mechanisms for gray areas that arise. This is already happening. As experience grows, bundled payments will become more comprehensive and inclusive. And a large body of evidence shows that the effort involved in understanding full care cycles and moving to multidisciplinary care is well worth it.

Why DRGs Are Not Bundled Payments

CRITICS OF BUNDLED PAYMENTS point to Medicare's experience with a superficially similar approach: the diagnosis-related group, or DRG, payment model. DRGs, which date back to 1984 and were adopted in many countries, were a step forward, but they did not trigger the hoped-for innovations in care delivery.

Why have DRGs failed to bring about greater change? DRGs make a single payment for a set of services provided at a given location; however, the payment does not cover the full care cycle for treating the patient's condition. By continuing to make separate payments to each specialist physician, hospital, and post-acute care site involved in a patient's care, DRGs perpetuate a system of uncoordinated care.

Moreover, DRG payments are not contingent on achieving good patient outcomes. Indeed, many DRGs fail to cover many support services crucial to good outcomes and overall value, such as patient education and counseling, behavioral health, and systematic follow-up. Under the DRG system, therefore, specialty silos in health care delivery have remained largely intact. And providers continue to have no incentive to innovate to improve patient outcomes.

Providers won't work together

Critics argue that bundled payments hold providers accountable for care by other providers that they don't control; skeptics also claim that it will be hard to divide up a single payment to fairly recognize each party's contribution. This is one reason many hospital systems have been slow to embrace the new payment model. We are selling doctors short. Many physician groups have enthusiastically embraced bundles, because they see how the model rewards great care, motivates collaboration, and brings clinicians together. As physicians form condition-based IPUs and develop mechanisms for sharing accountability, formulas for dividing revenues and risk are emerging that reflect each provider's role, rather than flawed legacy fee structures.

At UCLA's kidney transplant program, for example, a bundled payment was first negotiated with several insurers more than 20 years ago. An IPU was formed and has become one of the premier U.S. kidney transplantation programs with superior outcomes. To divide the bundled price, urologists and nephrologists—the specialists who have the greatest impact on care—pay negotiated fees to other specialists involved in care (such as anesthesiology) and bear the residual financial risk and share the gain. This structure has reinforced collaboration, not complicated it.

Another example is physician-owned OrthoCarolina's 2014 contract with Blue Cross and Blue Shield of North Carolina for bundled payment for joint replacement. OrthoCarolina provides care in several area hospitals and has negotiated a fixed payment with each of them for all the required inpatient care. Each participating hospital now has a designated team, including members of the nursing, quality, and administrative departments, that collaborates with OrthoCarolina surgeons in a virtual IPU. This ensures that everyone involved with the patient and the family fully understands the care pathway and expectations. The initial group of 220 patients in the plan experienced 0% readmissions, 0% reoperations, 0.45% deep venous thrombosis (versus 1% to 1.5% nationally), and substantial improvements in patient-reported quality-of-life outcomes. Average length of stay dropped from 2.4 days to 1.5 days, with 100% of patients discharged to their homes rather than a rehabilitation center. The cost per patient, as reported by Blue Cross and Blue Shield of North Carolina, fell an average of 20%.

Outcomes are difficult to measure

Critics claim that the outcome data at the medical condition level, an essential component of value-based bundled payments, doesn't exist or is too difficult and expensive to collect. While this may have been true a decade ago, today outcome measurement is rapidly expanding, including patient-reported outcomes covering functional results crucial to patients. Many providers are already systematically measuring outcomes. Martini-Klinik, a high-volume IPU for prostate cancer in Hamburg, Germany, has been measuring a broad set of outcomes since its founding, in 1994. This has enabled it to achieve complication rates for impotence and incontinence that are far lower than average for Germany. In congenital heart disease care, Texas Children's tracks not only risk-adjusted surgical and intensive care mortality rates but also metrics of patients' neurodevelopmental status and, increasingly, ongoing quality of life.

Advances in information technology are making outcome measurement better, easier, less costly, and more reliable. Greater standardization of the set of outcomes to measure by condition will also make measurement more efficient and improve benchmarking. The International Consortium for Health Outcomes Measurement (ICHOM) has published global standard sets of outcomes and risk factors for 21 medical conditions that represent a significant portion of the disease burden, and the number is growing. Early bundled payment programs are already achieving significant outcome improvement. As provider experience grows, bundled payments will expand accountability and lead to even greater improvements.

Current cost information is inadequate

Critics argue that bundled payments require an understanding of costs that most providers lack, which puts them at unfair financial risk. Yet numerous bundled payment programs are already in place, using prices based on modest discounts from the sum of historical fee-for-service payments. New service companies are assisting providers in aggregating past charges and in reducing costs. Providers will learn to measure their actual costs, as organizations such as Mayo Clinic, MD Anderson, and the University of Utah are already doing. This will inform better price negotiations and accelerate cost reduction.

The failure of care delivery organizations to properly measure and manage costs is a crucial weakness in health care globally. Bundled payments will finally motivate providers to master proper costing and use cost data to drive efficiencies without sacrificing good patient outcomes.

Providers will cherry-pick patients

Critics charge that bundled payments will encourage providers to treat only the easiest and healthiest patients. But as we have already noted, proper bundled payments are risk-stratified or risk-adjusted. Even today's imperfect bundled payment contracts incorporate risk adjustments that are often better than those used in current FFS payment and beyond the crude risk adjustment used in capitation. Innovators are developing pragmatic approaches that adjust for risk, such as restricting initial bundles to groups of patients with similar risk profiles for a condition. The County of Stockholm did this with joint replacements. Its initial bundle covered the 60% to 70% of patients classified as ASA 1 (normally healthy) or 2 (mild systemic disease); more-complex patients remained in the old reimbursement system. Careful tracking showed no evidence of bias in the selection of patients. The county plans to extend the bundle to more-complex joint replacement patients as better data becomes available.

Recently, the county introduced bundled payments for nine spine diagnoses requiring surgery, with far more sophisticated risk adjustment. The bundled payment includes a base payment, a payment covering expected complications, and a performance payment based on pain reduction. All three elements are adjusted for multiple patient risk factors. Risk adjustment will only improve as experience with it grows.

Bundled payments will encourage overtreatment

Critics raise concerns that bundled payments, like FFS, will lead to overtreatment because payment is tied to performing care, incenting providers to manufacture demand. Note that capitation plans, which have limited accountability for individual patient outcomes, have the opposite incentive: motivating providers to deny or delay the treatments patients need.

While definitive results are not yet available, our conversations with payers and government authorities in the United States, Sweden, and elsewhere have revealed no evidence that bundled payments have resulted in unnecessary surgeries or other treatments. Bundled payments are risk-adjusted and introduce transparency on outcomes, and the fixed payment will discourage unnecessary procedures, tests, and other services. Bundled payments (and all care) should incorporate appropriate use criteria (AUC), which use scientific evidence to define qualifications for particular treatments.

Price competition will trigger a race to the bottom
Finally, some providers worry that bundled payments will result in excessive price competition, as payers demand discounts and low-quality providers emerge offering cheap prices. This concern is common among hospitals, which are wary of greater competition and want to sustain existing reimbursement levels. We believe this fear is overblown. Bundled payments include clear accountability for outcomes and will penalize poor-quality providers. At the root of all these objections to bundled payments are critical failures that have held back health care for decades. Bundled payments will finally address these problems in ways that capitation cannot.

How Bundled Payments Will Transform Competition

As our multiple examples reveal, bundled payments are already transforming the way care is delivered. They unleash a new kind of competition that improves value for patients, informs and expands patient choice, lowers system cost, reshapes provider strategy, and alters industry structure for the better.

With bundled payments, patients are no longer locked into a single health system and can choose the provider that best meets their particular needs. Choice will expand dramatically as patients (and physicians) gain visibility into outcomes and prices of the providers that treat their condition. In a transparent bundled-payment world, patients will be able to decide whether to go to the hospital next door, travel across town, or venture even farther to a regional center of excellence for the care they need. This kind of choice, long overdue in health care, is what customers have in every other industry.

At the same time, the prices should fall. A bundled payment will usually be lower than the sum of current FFS reimbursements in today's inefficient and fragmented system. For conditions where legacy FFS payments failed to cover essential costs to achieve good outcomes, such as in mental health care or diagnostics that enable more targeted and successful treatments, prices may initially rise to support better care. But even these prices will fall as providers become more efficient.

In a world of bundled payments, market forces will determine provider prices and profitability, as they should. In today's system, FFS pricing allows inefficient or ineffective providers to be viable. With bundled payments, only providers that are effective and efficient will grow, earn attractive margins, and expand regionally and even nationally. The rest will see their margins decline, and those with poor outcomes will lose patients and bear the extra costs of dealing with avoidable complications, infections, readmissions, and repeat treatments.

Given today's hyperfragmentation of care, bundled payments should reduce the absolute number of providers treating each condition. But those that remain will be far stronger. And unlike the consolidation that would result from capitation, this winnowing of providers will create more-effective competition and greater accountability for results.

Providers will stop trying to do a little bit of everything and instead will target conditions where they can achieve good outcomes at low costs. Where they cannot, they will partner with more-effective providers or exit those service lines. The net result will be significantly better overall outcomes by condition and significantly lower average costs. No other payment model can produce such a transformation.

The shift to bundled payments will also spill over to drive positive change in pharmaceuticals, medical devices, diagnostic testing, imaging, and other suppliers. Today, suppliers compete to get on approved lists, curry favor with prescribing specialists through consulting and research payments, and advertise directly to patients so that they will ask their doctor for particular treatments. As a result, many patients receive therapies that are not the best option, deliver little benefit, or are unnecessary. With bundled payments, suppliers will have to demonstrate that their particular drug, device, diagnostic test, or imaging method actually improves outcomes, lowers the overall cost, or both. Suppliers that can demonstrate value will command fair prices and gain market share, and there will be substantial cost reduction in the system overall. Competition on value is the best way to control the costs of expensive drugs and therapies, not today's approach of restricting access or attacking high prices as unethical or evil regardless of the value products offer.

The Time Is Now

The biggest beneficiary of bundled payments will be patients, who will receive better care and have access to more choice. The best providers will also prosper. Many already recognize that bundled payments enable them to compete on value, transform care, and put the system on a sustainable health care path for the long run. Those already organized into IPUs for specific medical conditions are particularly well-positioned to move aggressively. Physician groups in particular have often moved the fastest.

Many health systems, however, have been reluctant to get behind bundled payments. They seem to believe that capitation better preserves the status quo—a top-down approach that leverages their clout and scale. They also see it as encouraging industry consolidation, which will ease reimbursement pressure and reduce competition. However, leading health systems are embracing bundled payments and the shift in competition to what really matters to patients.

Health systems with their own insurance plans, or those that self-insure care for their employees, can begin immediately to introduce bundled payments internally. Health systems that have adopted ACOs or other capitated models can also use condition-based bundled payments to pay internal units. Doing so will accelerate learning while motivating clinical units to improve outcomes and reduce costs in a way that existing departmental budgets or FFS can never match. Adopting bundles internally will be a stepping stone to contracting this way with payers and directly with employers.

Payers will reap huge benefits from bundled payments. Single-payer systems, such as those in Canada, Sweden, and the U.S. Veterans Administration, are well-positioned to transition to bundled payments for a growing number of medical conditions. Indeed, this is already happening in some countries and regions, with CMS leading the way in the United States.

But many private insurers, which have prospered under the status quo, have been disappointingly slow in moving to bundled payments. Many seem to favor capitation as less of a change; they believe it preserves payment infrastructure while shifting risk to providers. As an excuse, they cite their inability to process claims for bundled payments, even though bundled claims processing is inherently far simpler.

Improving the way they pay for health care, however, is the only means by which insurers can offer greater value to its customers. Insurers must do so, or they will have a diminished role in the system. We challenge the industry to shift from being the obstacle to bundled payment to becoming the driver. Recently, we've been heartened to see more private insurers moving toward bundled payments.

Employers, which actually pay for much of health insurance in the United States, should step up to lead the move to bundled payments. This will improve outcomes for their employees, bring down prices, and increase competition. Self-insured employer health plans need to direct their plan administrators to roll out bundles, starting with costly conditions for which employees experience uneven outcomes.

Should their insurers fail to move toward bundles, large employers have the clout to go directly to providers. Lowe's, Boeing, and Walmart are contracting directly with providers such as Mayo Clinic, Cleveland Clinic, Virginia Mason, and Geisinger on bundled payments for orthopedics and complex cardiac care. The Health Transformation Alliance, consisting of 20 large employers that account for 4 million lives, is pooling data and purchasing power to accelerate the implementation of bundled payments.

The time has come to change the way we pay for health care, in the United States and around the world. Capitation is not the solution. It entrenches large existing systems, eliminates patient choice, promotes more consolidation, limits competition, and perpetuates the lack of provider accountability for outcomes. It will fail again to drive true innovation in health care delivery.

Capitation will also fail to stem the tide of the ever-rising costs of health care. ACOs, despite their strong advocates, have produced minimal cost savings (0.1%). By contrast, even the simplified bundled payment contracts under way today are achieving better results. Medicare is expected to save at least 2% ($250 million) in its program's first full year of operation. And experience in the United States and elsewhere shows that the savings can be far larger.

Capitation might seem simple, but given highly heterogeneous populations and continual turnover of patients and physicians, it is actually harder to implement, risk-adjust, and manage to deliver improved care. Bundled payments, in contrast, are a direct and intuitive way to pay clinical teams for delivering value, condition by condition. They put accountability where it should be—on outcomes that matter to patients. This way to pay for health care is working, and expanding rapidly.

Much remains to be done to put bundled payments into widespread practice, but the barriers are rapidly being overcome. Bundled payments are the only true value-based payment model for health care. The time is now.

Further Reading

- **"The Strategy That Will Fix Health Care,"** Michael E. Porter and Thomas H. Lee, HBR, October 2013

- **"What Is Value in Health Care?,"** Michael E. Porter, *New England Journal of Medicine,* December 2010

- **"How to Solve the Cost Crisis in Health Care,"** Robert S. Kaplan and Michael E. Porter, HBR, September 2011

- **"Redesigning Primary Care: A Strategic Vision to Improve Value by Organizing Around Patients' Needs,"** Michael E. Porter, Erika A. Pabo, and Thomas H. Lee, *Health Affairs,* March 2013

- **"Getting Bundled Payments Right in Health Care,"** Derek A. Haas, Robert S. Kaplan, Dereesa Reid, Jonathan Warsh, and Michael E. West, HBR.org, October 2015

Originally published in July–August 2016. Reprint R1607G

The Performance Management Revolution

by Peter Cappelli and Anna Tavis

WHEN BRIAN JENSEN TOLD HIS AUDIENCE of HR executives that Colorcon wasn't bothering with annual reviews anymore, they were appalled. This was in 2002, during his tenure as the drugmaker's head of global human resources. In his presentation at the Wharton School, Jensen explained that Colorcon had found a more effective way of reinforcing desired behaviors and managing performance: Supervisors were giving people instant feedback, tying it to individuals' own goals, and handing out small weekly bonuses to employees they saw doing good things.

Back then the idea of abandoning the traditional appraisal process—and all that followed from it—seemed heretical. But now, by some estimates, more than one-third of U.S. companies are doing just that. From Silicon Valley to New York, and in offices across the world, firms are replacing annual reviews with frequent, informal check-ins between managers and employees.

As you might expect, technology companies such as Adobe, Juniper Systems, Dell, Microsoft, and IBM have led the way. Yet they've been joined by a number of professional services firms (Deloitte, Accenture, PwC), early adopters in other industries (Gap, Lear, OppenheimerFunds), and even General Electric, the longtime role model for traditional appraisals.

Without question, rethinking performance management is at the top of many executive teams' agendas, but what drove the change in this direction? Many factors. In a recent article for *People + Strategy,* a Deloitte manager referred to the review process as "an investment of 1.8 million hours across the firm that didn't fit our business needs anymore." One *Washington Post* business writer called it a "rite of corporate kabuki" that restricts creativity, generates mountains of paperwork, and serves no real purpose. Others have described annual reviews as a last-century practice and blamed them for a lack of collaboration and innovation. Employers are also finally acknowledging that both supervisors and subordinates despise the appraisal process—a perennial problem that feels more urgent now that the labor market is picking up and concerns about retention have returned.

But the biggest limitation of annual reviews—and, we have observed, the main reason more and more companies are dropping them—is this: With their heavy emphasis on financial rewards and punishments and their end-of-year structure, they hold people accountable for past behavior at the expense of improving current performance and grooming talent for the future, both of which are critical for organizations' long-term survival. In contrast, regular conversations about performance and development change the focus to building the workforce your organization needs to be competitive both today and years from now. Business researcher Josh Bersin estimates that about 70% of multinational companies are moving toward this model, even if they haven't arrived quite yet.

The tension between the traditional and newer approaches stems from a long-running dispute about managing people: Do you "get what you get" when you hire your employees? Should you focus mainly on motivating the strong ones with money and getting rid of the weak ones? Or are employees malleable? Can you change the way they perform through effective coaching and management and intrinsic rewards such as personal growth and a sense of progress on the job?

With traditional appraisals, the pendulum had swung too far toward the former, more transactional view of performance, which became hard to support in an era of low inflation and tiny merit-pay budgets. Those who still hold that view are railing against the recent

Idea in Brief

The Problem

By emphasizing individual accountability for past results, traditional appraisals give short shrift to improving current performance and developing talent for the future. That can hinder long-term competitiveness.

The Solution

To better support employee development, many organizations are dropping or radically changing their annual review systems in favor of giving people less formal, more frequent feedback that follows the natural cycle of work.

The Outlook

This shift isn't just a fad—real business needs are driving it. Support at the top is critical, though. Some firms that have struggled to go entirely without ratings are trying a "third way": assigning multiple ratings several times a year to encourage employees' growth.

emphasis on improvement and growth over accountability. But the new perspective is unlikely to be a flash in the pan because, as we will discuss, it is being driven by business needs, not imposed by HR.

First, though, let's consider how we got to this point—and how companies are faring with new approaches.

How We Got Here

Historical and economic context has played a large role in the evolution of performance management over the decades. When human capital was plentiful, the focus was on which people to let go, which to keep, and which to reward—and for those purposes, traditional appraisals (with their emphasis on individual accountability) worked pretty well. But when talent was in shorter supply, as it is now, developing people became a greater concern—and organizations had to find new ways of meeting that need.

From accountability to development

Appraisals can be traced back to the U.S. military's "merit rating" system, created during World War I to identify poor performers for discharge or transfer. After World War II, about 60% of U.S. companies were using them (by the 1960s, it was closer to 90%). Though seniority rules determined pay increases and promotions for unionized workers, strong merit scores meant good advancement prospects for managers. At least initially, *improving* performance was an afterthought.

And then a severe shortage of managerial talent caused a shift in organizational priorities: Companies began using appraisals to develop employees into supervisors, and especially managers into executives. In a famous 1957 HBR article, social psychologist Douglas McGregor argued that subordinates should, with feedback from the boss, help set their performance goals and assess themselves—a process that would build on their strengths and potential. This "Theory Y" approach to management—he coined the term later on—assumed that employees wanted to perform well and would do so if supported properly. ("Theory X" assumed you had to motivate people with material rewards and punishments.) McGregor noted one drawback to the approach he advocated: Doing it right would take managers several days per subordinate each year.

By the early 1960s, organizations had become so focused on developing future talent that many observers thought that tracking past performance had fallen by the wayside. Part of the problem was that supervisors were reluctant to distinguish good performers from bad. One study, for example, found that 98% of federal government employees received "satisfactory" ratings, while only 2% got either of the other two outcomes: "unsatisfactory" or "outstanding." After running a well-publicized experiment in 1964, General Electric concluded it was best to split the appraisal process into separate discussions about accountability and development, given the conflicts between them. Other companies followed suit.

Back to accountability

In the 1970s, however, a shift began. Inflation rates shot up, and merit-based pay took center stage in the appraisal process. During that period, annual wage increases really mattered. Supervisors often had discretion to give raises of 20% or more to strong performers, to distinguish them from the sea of employees receiving basic cost-of-living raises, and getting no increase represented a substantial pay cut. With the stakes so high—and with antidiscrimination laws so recently on the books—the pressure was on to award pay more objectively. As a result, accountability became a higher priority than development for many organizations.

Three other changes in the zeitgeist reinforced that shift:

First, Jack Welch became CEO of General Electric in 1981. To deal with the long-standing concern that supervisors failed to label real differences in performance, Welch championed the forced-ranking system—another military creation. Though the U.S. Army had devised it, just before entering World War II, to quickly identify a large number of officer candidates for the country's imminent military expansion, GE used it to shed people at the bottom. Equating performance with individuals' inherent capabilities (and largely ignoring their potential to grow), Welch divided his workforce into "A" players, who must be rewarded; "B" players, who should be accommodated; and "C" players, who should be dismissed. In that system, development was reserved for the "A" players—the high-potentials chosen to advance into senior positions.

Second, 1993 legislation limited the tax deductibility of executive salaries to $1 million but exempted performance-based pay. That led to a rise in outcome-based bonuses for corporate leaders—a change that trickled down to frontline managers and even hourly employees—and organizations relied even more on the appraisal process to assess merit.

Third, McKinsey's War for Talent research project in the late 1990s suggested that some employees were fundamentally more talented than others (you knew them when you saw them, the thinking went). Because such individuals were, by definition, in short supply, organizations felt they needed to take great care in tracking and rewarding them. Nothing in the McKinsey studies showed that fixed personality traits actually made certain people perform better, but that was the assumption.

So, by the early 2000s, organizations were using performance appraisals mainly to hold employees accountable and to allocate rewards. By some estimates, as many as one-third of U.S. corporations—and 60% of the *Fortune* 500—had adopted a forced-ranking system. At the same time, other changes in corporate life made it harder for the appraisal process to advance the time-consuming goals of improving individual performance and developing skills for future roles. Organizations got much flatter, which dramatically increased the number of subordinates that supervisors had to manage. The new norm was 15 to 25 direct reports (up from six before the 1960s). While overseeing more employees, supervisors were also expected to be individual contributors. So taking days to manage the performance issues of each employee, as Douglas McGregor had advocated, was impossible. Meanwhile, greater interest in lateral hiring reduced the need for internal development. Up to two-thirds of corporate jobs were filled from outside, compared with about 10% a generation earlier.

Back to development . . . again

Another major turning point came in 2005: A few years after Jack Welch left GE, the company quietly backed away from forced ranking because it fostered internal competition and undermined collaboration. Welch still defends the practice, but what he really supports is the general principle of letting people know how they are doing: "As a manager, you owe candor to your people," he wrote in the *Wall Street Journal* in 2013. "They must not be guessing about what the organization thinks of them." It's hard to argue against candor, of course. But more and more firms began questioning how useful it was to compare people with one another or even to rate them on a scale.

So the emphasis on accountability for past performance started to fade. That continued as jobs became more complex and rapidly changed shape—in that climate, it was difficult to set annual goals that would still be meaningful 12 months later. Plus, the move toward team-based work often conflicted with individual appraisals and rewards. And low inflation and small budgets for wage increases made appraisal-driven merit pay seem futile. What was the point of trying to draw performance distinctions when rewards were so trivial?

The whole appraisal process was loathed by employees anyway. Social science research showed that they hated numerical scores—they would rather be told they were "average" than given a 3 on a

5-point scale. They especially detested forced ranking. As Wharton's Iwan Barankay demonstrated in a field setting, performance actually declined when people were rated relative to others. Nor did the ratings seem accurate. As the accumulating research on appraisal scores showed, they had as much to do with who the rater was (people gave higher ratings to those who were like them) as they did with performance.

And managers hated *doing* reviews, as survey after survey made clear. Willis Towers Watson found that 45% did not see value in the systems they used. Deloitte reported that 58% of HR executives considered reviews an ineffective use of supervisors' time. In a study by the advisory service CEB, the average manager reported spending about 210 hours—close to five weeks—doing appraisals each year.

As dissatisfaction with the traditional process mounted, high-tech firms ushered in a new way of thinking about performance. The "Agile Manifesto," created by software developers in 2001, outlined several key values—favoring, for instance, "responding to change over following a plan." It emphasized principles such as collaboration, self-organization, self-direction, and regular reflection on how to work more effectively, with the aim of prototyping more quickly and responding in real time to customer feedback and changes in requirements. Although not directed at performance per se, these principles changed the definition of effectiveness on the job—and they were at odds with the usual practice of cascading goals from the top down and assessing people against them once a year.

So it makes sense that the first significant departure from traditional reviews happened at Adobe, in 2011. The company was already using the agile method, breaking down projects into "sprints" that were immediately followed by debriefing sessions. Adobe explicitly brought this notion of constant assessment and feedback into performance management, with frequent check-ins replacing annual appraisals. Juniper Systems, Dell, and Microsoft were prominent followers.

CEB estimated in 2014 that 12% of U.S. companies had dropped annual reviews altogether. Willis Towers Watson put the figure at 8% but added that 29% were considering eliminating them or planning to do so. Deloitte reported in 2015 that only 12% of the U.S. companies it surveyed were *not* planning to rethink their performance management systems. This trend seems to be extending beyond the United States as well. PwC reports that two-thirds of large companies in the UK, for example, are in the process of changing their systems.

Three Business Reasons to Drop Appraisals

In light of that history, we see three clear business imperatives that are leading companies to abandon performance appraisals:

The return of people development

Companies are under competitive pressure to upgrade their talent management efforts. This is especially true at consulting and other professional services firms, where knowledge work is the offering—and where inexperienced college grads are turned into skilled advisers through structured training. Such firms are doubling down on development, often by putting their employees (who are deeply motivated by the potential for learning and advancement) in charge of their own growth. This approach requires rich feedback from supervisors—a need that's better met by frequent, informal check-ins than by annual reviews.

Now that the labor market has tightened and keeping good people is once again critical, such companies have been trying to eliminate "dissatisfiers" that drive employees away. Naturally, annual reviews are on that list, since the process is so widely reviled and the focus on numerical ratings interferes with the learning that people want and need to do. Replacing this system with feedback that's delivered right after client engagements helps managers do a better job of coaching and allows subordinates to process and apply the advice more effectively.

Kelly Services was the first big professional services firm to drop appraisals, in 2011. PwC tried it with a pilot group in 2013 and then discontinued annual reviews for all 200,000-plus employees. Deloitte followed in 2015, and Accenture and KPMG made similar announcements shortly thereafter. Given the sheer size of these firms, and the fact that they offer management advice to thousands of organizations, their choices are having an enormous impact on other companies. Firms that scrap appraisals are also rethinking employee management much more broadly. Accenture CEO Pierre Nanterme estimates that his firm is changing about 90% of its talent practices.

The need for agility

When rapid innovation is a source of competitive advantage, as it is now in many companies and industries, that means future needs are continually changing. Because organizations won't necessarily want employees to keep doing the same things, it doesn't make sense to hang on to a system that's built mainly to assess and hold people accountable for past or current practices. As Susan Peters, GE's head of human resources, has pointed out, businesses no longer have clear annual cycles. Projects are short-term and tend to change along the way, so employees' goals and tasks can't be plotted out a year in advance with much accuracy.

At GE a new business strategy based on innovation was the biggest reason the company recently began eliminating individual ratings and annual reviews. Its new approach to performance management is aligned with its FastWorks platform for creating products and bringing them to market, which borrows a lot from agile techniques. Supervisors still have an end-of-year summary discussion with subordinates, but the goal is to push frequent conversations with employees (GE calls them "touchpoints") and keep revisiting two basic questions: What am I doing that I should keep doing? And what am I doing that I should change? Annual goals have been replaced with shorter-term "priorities." As with many of the companies we see, GE first launched a pilot, with about 87,000 employees in 2015, before adopting the changes across the company.

The centrality of teamwork

Moving away from forced ranking and from appraisals' focus on individual accountability makes it easier to foster teamwork. This has become especially clear at retail companies like Sears and Gap—perhaps the most surprising early innovators in appraisals. Sophisticated customer service now requires frontline and back-office employees to work together to keep shelves stocked and manage customer flow, and traditional systems don't enhance performance at the team level or help track collaboration.

Gap supervisors still give workers end-of-year assessments, but only to summarize performance discussions that happen throughout the year and to set pay increases accordingly. Employees still have goals, but as at other companies, the goals are short-term (in this case, quarterly). Now two years into its new system, Gap reports far more satisfaction with its performance process and the best-ever completion of store-level goals. Nonetheless, Rob Ollander-Krane, Gap's senior director of organization performance effectiveness, says the company needs further improvement in setting stretch goals and focusing on team performance.

Implications

All three reasons for dropping annual appraisals argue for a system that more closely follows the natural cycle of work. Ideally, conversations between managers and employees occur when projects finish, milestones are reached, challenges pop up, and so forth—allowing people to solve problems in current performance while also developing skills for the future. At most companies, managers take the lead in setting near-term goals, and employees drive career conversations throughout the year. In the words of one Deloitte manager: "The conversations are more holistic. They're about goals and strengths, not just about past performance."

Perhaps most important, companies are overhauling performance management because their businesses require the change. That's true whether they're professional services firms that must develop people in order to compete, companies that need to deliver ongoing performance feedback to support rapid innovation, or retailers that need better coordination between the sales floor and the back office to serve their customers.

Of course, many HR managers worry: If we can't get supervisors to have good conversations with subordinates once a year, how can we expect them to do so more frequently, without the support of the usual appraisal process? It's a valid question—but we see reasons to be optimistic.

As GE found in 1964 and as research has documented since, it is extraordinarily difficult to have a serious, open discussion about problems while also dishing out consequences such as low merit pay. The end-of-year review was also an excuse for delaying feedback until then, at which point both the supervisor and the employee were likely to have forgotten what had happened months earlier. Both of those constraints disappear when you take away the annual review. Additionally, almost all companies that have dropped traditional appraisals have invested in training supervisors to talk more about development with their employees—and they are checking with subordinates to make sure that's happening.

Moving to an informal system requires a culture that will keep the continuous feedback going. As Megan Taylor, Adobe's director of business partnering, pointed out at a recent conference, it's difficult to sustain that if it's not happening organically. Adobe, which has gone totally numberless but still gives merit increases based on informal assessments, reports that regular conversations between managers and their employees are now occurring without HR's prompting. Deloitte, too, has found that its new model of frequent, informal check-ins has led to more meaningful discussions, deeper insights, and greater employee satisfaction. (For more details, see "Reinventing Performance Management," HBR, April 2015.) The firm started to go numberless like Adobe but then switched to assigning employees several numbers four times a year, to give them rolling feedback on different dimensions. Jeffrey Orlando, who heads up development and performance at Deloitte, says the company has been tracking the effects on business results, and they've been positive so far.

Challenges That Persist

The greatest resistance to abandoning appraisals, which is something of a revolution in human resources, comes from HR itself. The reason is simple: Many of the processes and systems that HR has built over the years revolve around those performance ratings. Experts in employment law had advised organizations to standardize practices, develop objective criteria to justify every employment decision, and

A talent management timeline

The tug-of-war between accountability and development over the decades

WWI	WWII	1940s	1950s	1960s	1970s
The U.S. military created merit-rating system to flag and dismiss poor performers.	The Army devised forced ranking to identify enlisted soldiers with the potential to become officers.	About 60% of U.S. companies were using appraisals to document workers' performance and allocate rewards.	Social psychologist Douglas McGregor argued for engaging employees in assessments and goal setting.	Led by General Electric, companies began splitting appraisals into separate discussions about accountability and growth, to give development its due.	Inflation rates shot up, and organizations felt pressure to award merit pay more objectively, so accountability again became the priority in the appraisal process.

1980s

Jack Welch championed forced ranking at GE to reward top performers, accommodate those in the middle, and get rid of those at the bottom.

1990s

McKinsey's War for Talent study pointed to a shortage of capable executives and reinforced the emphasis on assessing and rewarding performance.

2000

Organizations got flatter, which dramatically increased the number of direct reports each manager had, making it harder to invest time in developing them.

2011

Kelly Services was the first big professional services firm to drop appraisals, and other major firms followed suit, emphasizing frequent, informal feedback.

Adobe ended annual performance reviews, in keeping with the famous "Agile Manifesto" and the notion that annual targets were irrelevant to the way its business operated.

2016

Deloitte, PwC, and others that tried going numberless are reinstating performance ratings but using more than one number and keeping the new emphasis on developmental feedback.

☐ Accountability focus
⌐¬ Development focus
☐ A hybrid "third way"

document all relevant facts. Taking away appraisals flies in the face of that advice—and it doesn't necessarily solve every problem that they failed to address.

Here are some of the challenges that organizations still grapple with when they replace the old performance model with new approaches:

Aligning individual and company goals

In the traditional model, business objectives and strategies cascaded down the organization. All the units, and then all the individual employees, were supposed to establish their goals to reflect and reinforce the direction set at the top. But this approach works only when business goals are easy to articulate and held constant over the course of a year. As we've discussed, that's often not the case these days, and employee goals may be pegged to specific projects. So as projects unfold and tasks change, how do you coordinate individual priorities with the goals for the whole enterprise, especially when the business objectives are short-term and must rapidly adapt to market shifts? It's a new kind of problem to solve, and the jury is still out on how to respond.

Rewarding performance

Appraisals gave managers a clear-cut way of tying rewards to individual contributions. Companies changing their systems are trying to figure out how their new practices will affect the pay-for-performance model, which none of them have explicitly abandoned.

They still differentiate rewards, usually relying on managers' qualitative judgments rather than numerical ratings. In pilot programs at Juniper Systems and Cargill, supervisors had no difficulty allocating merit-based pay without appraisal scores. In fact, both line managers and HR staff felt that paying closer attention to employee performance throughout the year was likely to make their merit-pay decisions more valid.

But it will be interesting to see whether most supervisors end up reviewing the feedback they've given each employee over the year before determining merit increases. (Deloitte's managers already do this.) If so, might they produce something *like* an annual appraisal score—even though it's more carefully considered? And could that subtly undermine development by shifting managers' focus back to accountability?

Identifying poor performers

Though managers may assume they need appraisals to determine which employees aren't doing their jobs well, the traditional process doesn't *really* help much with that. For starters, individuals' ratings jump around over time. Research shows that last year's performance score predicts only one-third of the variance in this year's score—so it's hard to say that someone simply isn't up to scratch. Plus, HR departments consistently complain that line managers don't use the appraisal process to document poor performers. Even when they do, waiting until the end of the year to flag struggling employees allows failure to go on for too long without intervention.

We've observed that companies that have dropped appraisals are requiring supervisors to immediately identify problem employees. Juniper Systems also formally asks supervisors each quarter to confirm that their subordinates are performing up to company standards. Only 3%, on average, are not, and HR is brought in to address them. Adobe reports that its new system has reduced dismissals, because struggling employees are monitored and coached much more closely.

Still, given how reluctant most managers are to single out failing employees, we can't assume that getting rid of appraisals will make those tough calls any easier. And all the companies we've observed still have "performance improvement plans" for employees identified as needing support. Such plans remain universally problematic, too, partly because many issues that cause poor performance can't be solved by management intervention.

Avoiding legal troubles

Employee relations managers within HR often worry that discrimination charges will spike if their companies stop basing pay increases and promotions on numerical ratings, which seem objective. But appraisals haven't prevented discriminatory practices. Though they force managers to systematically review people's contributions each year, a great deal of discretion (always subject to bias) is built into the process, and considerable evidence shows that supervisors discriminate against some employees by giving them undeservedly low ratings.

Leaders at Gap report that their new practices were driven partly by complaints and research showing that the appraisal process was often biased and ineffective. Frontline workers in retail (disproportionately women and minorities) are especially vulnerable to unfair treatment. Indeed, formal ratings may do more to *reveal* bias than to curb it. If a company has clear appraisal scores and merit-pay indexes, it is easy to see if women and minorities with the same scores as white men are getting fewer or lower pay increases.

All that said, it's not clear that new approaches to performance management will do much to mitigate discrimination either. (See the sidebar "Can You Take Cognitive Bias Out of Assessments?") Gap has found that getting rid of performance scores increased fairness in pay and other decisions, but judgments still have to be made—and there's the possibility of bias in every piece of qualitative information that decision makers consider.

Managing the feedback firehose

In recent years most HR information systems were built to move annual appraisals online and connect them to pay increases, succession planning, and so forth. They weren't designed to accommodate continuous feedback, which is one reason many employee check-ins consist of oral comments, with no documentation.

The tech world has responded with apps that enable supervisors to give feedback anytime and to record it if desired. At General Electric, the PD@GE app ("PD" stands for "performance development") allows managers to call up notes and materials from prior conversations and summarize that information. Employees can use the app to ask for direction when they need it. IBM has a similar app that adds another feature: It enables employees to give feedback to peers and choose whether the recipient's boss gets a copy. Amazon's

Can You Take Cognitive Bias out of Assessments?

A CLASSIC STUDY BY EDWARD JONES and Victor Harris in the 1960s demonstrated that people tend to attribute others' behavior to character rather than circumstances.

When a car goes streaking past us, for instance, we think that the driver is a jerk and ignore the possibility that there might be an emergency. A good workplace example of this cognitive bias—known as the "fundamental attribution error"—is to assume that the lowest performers in any year will always be the worst performers and to fire them as a result. Such an assumption overlooks the impact of good or poor management, not to mention business conditions that are beyond employees' control.

Of course, this model is highly flattering to people who have advanced into executive roles—"A" players whose success is, by definition, credited to their superior abilities, not to good fortune. That may be partly why the model has persisted so long in the face of considerable evidence against it.

Even when "A" players seem to perform well in many contexts (and that's rarely measured), they may be coasting on the "halo effect"—another type of bias, akin to self-fulfilling prophecy. If these folks have already been successful, they receive more opportunities than others, and they're pushed harder, so naturally they do better.

Biases color individual performance ratings as well. Decision makers may give past behavior too much weight, for instance, or fall prey to stereotypes when they assign their ratings.

But when you get rid of forced ranking and appraisal scores, you don't eradicate bias. Discrimination and faulty assumptions still creep into qualitative assessments. In some ways the older, more cumbersome performance systems actually made it harder for managers to keep their blinders on. Formal feedback from various stakeholders provided some balance when supervisors were otherwise inclined to see only the good things their stars did and failed to recognize others' contributions.

Anytime you exercise judgment, whether or not you translate that to numerical ratings, intuition plays a part, and bias can rear its head.

Anytime Feedback tool does much the same thing. The great advantage of these apps is that supervisors can easily review all the discussion text when it is time to take actions such as award merit pay or consider promotions and job reassignments.

Of course, being on the receiving end of all that continual coaching could get overwhelming—it never lets up. And as for peer feedback, it isn't always useful, even if apps make it easier to deliver in real time. Typically, it's less objective than supervisor feedback, as anyone familiar with 360s knows. It can be also "gamed" by employees to help or hurt colleagues. (At Amazon, the cutthroat culture encourages employees to be critical of one another's performance, and forced ranking creates an incentive to push others to the bottom of the heap.) The more consequential the peer feedback, the more likely the problems.

Not all employers face the same business pressures to change their performance processes. In some fields and industries (think sales and financial services), it still makes sense to emphasize accountability and financial rewards for individual performers. Organizations with a strong public mission may also be well served by traditional appraisals. But even government organizations like NASA and the FBI are rethinking their approach, having concluded that accountability should be collective and that supervisors need to do a better job of coaching and developing their subordinates.

Ideology at the top matters. Consider what happened at Intel. In a two-year pilot, employees got feedback but no formal appraisal scores. Though supervisors did not have difficulty differentiating performance or distributing performance-based pay without the ratings, company executives returned to using them, believing they created healthy competition and clear outcomes. At Sun Communities, a manufactured-home company, senior leaders also oppose eliminating appraisals because they think formal feedback is essential to accountability. And Medtronic, which gave up ratings several years ago, is resurrecting them now that it has acquired

Ireland-based Covidien, which has a more traditional view of performance management.

Other firms aren't completely reverting to old approaches but instead seem to be seeking middle ground. As we've mentioned, Deloitte has backpedaled from giving no ratings at all to having project leads and managers assign them in four categories on a quarterly basis, to provide detailed "performance snapshots." PwC recently made a similar move in its client-services practices: Employees still don't receive a single rating each year, but they now get scores on five competencies, along with other development feedback. In PwC's case, the pushback against going numberless actually came from employees, especially those on a partner track, who wanted to know how they were doing.

At one insurance company, after formal ratings had been eliminated, merit-pay increases were being shared internally and then interpreted as performance scores. These became known as "shadow ratings," and because they started to affect other talent management decisions, the company eventually went back to formal appraisals. But it kept other changes it had made to its performance management system, such as quarterly conversations between managers and employees, to maintain its new commitment to development.

It will be interesting to see how well these "third way" approaches work. They, too, could fail if they aren't supported by senior leadership and reinforced by organizational culture. Still, in most cases, sticking with old systems seems like a bad option. Companies that don't think an overhaul makes sense for them should at least carefully consider whether their process is giving them what they need to solve current performance problems and develop future talent. Performance appraisals wouldn't be the least popular practice in business, as they're widely believed to be, if *something* weren't fundamentally wrong with them.

Originally published in October 2016. Reprint R1610D

Let Your Workers Rebel

by Francesca Gino

THROUGHOUT OUR CAREERS, we are taught to conform—to the status quo, to the opinions and behaviors of others, and to information that supports our views. The pressure only grows as we climb the organizational ladder. By the time we reach high-level positions, conformity has been so hammered into us that we perpetuate it in our enterprises. In a recent survey I conducted of more than 2,000 employees across a wide range of industries, nearly half the respondents reported working in organizations where they regularly feel the need to conform, and more than half said that people in their organizations do not question the status quo. The results were similar when I surveyed high-level executives and midlevel managers. As this data suggests, organizations consciously or unconsciously urge employees to check a good chunk of their real selves at the door. Workers and their organizations both pay a price: decreased engagement, productivity, and innovation (see the exhibit "The perils of conformity").

Drawing on my research and fieldwork and on the work of other scholars of psychology and management, I will describe three reasons for our conformity on the job, discuss why this behavior is costly for organizations, and suggest ways to combat it.

Of course, not all conformity is bad. But to be successful and evolve, organizations need to strike a balance between adherence to the formal and informal rules that provide necessary structure and the freedom that helps employees do their best work. The pendulum has swung too far in the direction of conformity. In another recent survey I conducted, involving more than 1,000 employees in a variety of industries, less than 10% said they worked in companies that regularly encourage nonconformity. That's not surprising: For decades the principles of scientific management have prevailed. Leaders have been overly focused on designing efficient processes and getting employees to follow them. Now they need to think about when conformity hurts their business and allow—even promote— what I call *constructive nonconformity:* behavior that deviates from organizational norms, others' actions, or common expectations, to the benefit of the organization.

Why Conformity Is So Prevalent

Let's look at the three main, and interrelated, reasons why we so often conform at work.

We fall prey to social pressure

Early in life we learn that tangible benefits arise from following social rules about what to say, how to act, how to dress, and so on. Conforming makes us feel accepted and part of the majority. As classic research conducted in the 1950s by the psychologist Solomon Asch showed, conformity to peer pressure is so powerful that it occurs even when we know it will lead us to make bad decisions. In one experiment, Asch asked participants to complete what they believed was a simple perceptual task: identifying which of three lines on one card was the same length as a line on another card. When asked individually, participants chose the correct line. When asked in the presence of paid actors who intentionally selected the wrong line, about 75% conformed to the group at least once. In other words, they chose an incorrect answer in order to fit in.

Organizations have long exploited this tendency. Ancient Roman families employed professional mourners at funerals. Entertainment companies hire people ("claques") to applaud at performances. And companies advertising health products often report the percentage of doctors or dentists who use their offerings.

Conformity at work takes many forms: modeling the behavior of others in similar roles, expressing appropriate emotions, wearing proper attire, routinely agreeing with the opinions of managers, acquiescing to a team's poor decisions, and so on. And all too often, bowing to peer pressure reduces individuals' engagement with their jobs. This is understandable: Conforming often conflicts with our true preferences and beliefs and therefore makes us feel inauthentic. In fact, research I conducted with Maryam Kouchaki, of Northwestern University, and Adam Galinsky, of Columbia University, showed that when people feel inauthentic at work, it's usually because they have succumbed to social pressure to conform.

We become too comfortable with the status quo

In organizations, standard practices—the usual ways of thinking and doing—play a critical role in shaping performance over time. But they can also get us stuck, decrease our engagement, and constrain our ability to innovate or to perform at a high level. Rather than resulting from thoughtful choices, many traditions endure out of routine, or what psychologists call the *status quo bias*. Because we feel validated and reassured when we stick to our usual ways of thinking and doing, and because—as research has consistently found—we weight the potential losses of deviating from the status quo much more heavily than we do the potential gains, we favor decisions that maintain the current state of affairs.

But sticking with the status quo can lead to boredom, which in turn can fuel complacency and stagnation. Borders, BlackBerry, Polaroid, and Myspace are but a few of the many companies that once had winning formulas but didn't update their strategies until it was too late. Overly comfortable with the status quo, their leaders fell back on tradition and avoided the type of nonconformist behavior that could have spurred continued success.

We interpret information in a self-serving manner

A third reason for the prevalence of conformity is that we tend to prioritize information that supports our existing beliefs and to ignore information that challenges them, so we overlook things that could spur positive change. Complicating matters, we also tend to view unexpected or unpleasant information as a threat and to shun it—a phenomenon psychologists call *motivated skepticism.*

In fact, research suggests, the manner in which we weigh evidence resembles the manner in which we weigh ourselves on a bathroom scale. If the scale delivers bad news, we hop off and get back on—perhaps the scale misfired or we misread the display. If it delivers good news, we assume it's correct and cheerfully head for the shower.

Here's a more scientific example. Two psychologists, Peter Ditto and David Lopez, asked study participants to evaluate a student's intelligence by reviewing information about him one piece at a time—similar to the way college admissions officers evaluate applicants. The information was quite negative. Subjects could stop going through it as soon as they'd reached a firm conclusion. When they had been primed to like the student (with a photo and some information provided before the evaluation), they turned over one card after another, searching for anything that would allow them to give a favorable rating. When they had been primed to dislike him, they turned over a few cards, shrugged, and called it a day.

By uncritically accepting information when it is consistent with what we believe and insisting on more when it isn't, we subtly stack the deck against good decisions.

Promoting Constructive Nonconformity

Few leaders actively encourage deviant behavior in their employees; most go to great lengths to get rid of it. Yet nonconformity promotes innovation, improves performance, and can enhance a person's standing more than conformity can. For example, research I conducted with Silvia Bellezza, of Columbia, and Anat Keinan, of Harvard, showed that observers judge a keynote speaker who wears red sneakers, a CEO who makes the rounds of Wall Street in a hoodie and jeans, and a presenter who creates her own PowerPoint template rather than using her company's as having higher status than counterparts who conform to business norms.

My research also shows that going against the crowd gives us confidence in our actions, which makes us feel unique and engaged and translates to higher performance and greater creativity. In one field study, I asked a group of employees to behave in nonconforming ways (speaking up if they disagreed with colleagues' decisions, expressing what they felt rather than what they thought they were expected to feel, and so on). I asked another group to behave in conforming ways, and a third group to do whatever its members usually did. After three weeks, those in the first group reported feeling more confident and engaged in their work than those in the other groups. They displayed more creativity in a task that was part of the study. And their supervisors gave them higher ratings on performance and innovativeness.

Six strategies can help leaders encourage constructive nonconformity in their organizations and themselves.

Step 1: Give Employees Opportunities to Be Themselves

Decades' worth of psychological research has shown that we feel accepted and believe that our views are more credible when our colleagues share them. But although conformity may make us feel good, it doesn't let us reap the benefits of authenticity. In one study Dan Cable, of London Business School, and Virginia Kay, then of the University of North Carolina at Chapel Hill, surveyed 154 recent MBA graduates who were four months into their jobs. Those who felt they could express their authentic selves at work were, on average, 16% more engaged and more committed to their organizations than those who felt they had to hide their authentic selves. In another study, Cable and Kay surveyed 2,700 teachers who had been working for a year and reviewed the performance ratings given by their supervisors. Teachers who said they could express their authentic selves received higher ratings than teachers who did not feel they could do so.

Here are some ways to help workers be true to themselves:

Encourage employees to reflect on what makes them feel authentic. This can be done from the very start of the employment relationship—during orientation. In a field study I conducted with

The perils of conformity

Organizations put tremendous pressure on employees to conform. In a recent survey of 2,087 U.S. employees in a wide range of industries, nearly 49% agreed with the statement "I regularly feel pressure to conform in this organization."

This takes a heavy toll on individuals and enterprises alike. Employees who felt a need to conform reported a less positive work experience on several dimensions than did other employees, as shown by the average scores plotted below.

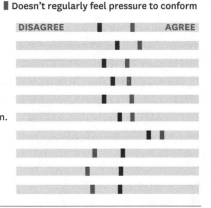

■ Regularly feels pressure to conform   ■ Doesn't regularly feel pressure to conform

	DISAGREE		AGREE
I can be myself at work.			
My organization fully uses my talents.			
I am committed to my organization.			
I am engaged in my work.			
I am satisfied with my job.			
I try to improve my job and my organization.			
I perform at a high level.			
I lack control over my job.			
I feel burned out.			
I would like to leave my organization.			

Brad Staats, of the University of North Carolina at Chapel Hill, and Dan Cable, employees in the business-process-outsourcing division of the Indian IT company Wipro went through a slightly modified onboarding process. We gave them a half hour to think about what was unique about them, what made them authentic, and how they could bring out their authentic selves at work. Later we compared them with employees who had gone through Wipro's usual onboarding program, which allowed no time for such reflection. The employees in the first group had found ways to tailor their jobs so that they could be their true selves—for example, they exercised judgment when answering calls instead of rigidly following the company script. They were more engaged in their work, performed better, and were more likely to be with the company seven months later.

Leaders can also encourage this type of reflection once people are on the job. The start of a new year is a natural time for employees and their leaders to reflect on what makes them unique and authentic and how they can shape their jobs—even in small ways—to avoid conformity. Reflection can also be encouraged at other career points, such as a performance review, a promotion, or a transition into a new role.

Tell employees what job needs to be done rather than how to do it. When Colleen Barrett was executive vice president of Southwest Airlines, from 1990 to 2001, she established the goal of allowing employees to be themselves. For example, flight attendants were encouraged to deliver the legally required safety announcement in their own style and with humor. "We have always thought that your avocation can be your vocation so that you don't have to do any acting in your life when you leave home to go to work," she has said. This philosophy helped make Southwest a top industry performer in terms of passenger volume, profitability, customer satisfaction, and turnover.

Let employees solve problems on their own. Leaders can encourage authenticity by allowing workers to decide how to handle certain situations. For instance, in the 1990s British Airways got rid of its thick customer-service handbook and gave employees the freedom (within reason) to figure out how to deal with customer problems as they arose (see "Competing on Customer Service: An Interview with British Airways' Sir Colin Marshall," HBR, November–December 1995).

Another company that subscribes to this philosophy is Pal's Sudden Service, a fast-food chain in the southern United States. By implementing lean principles, including the idea that workers are empowered to call out and fix problems, Pal's has achieved impressive numbers: one car served at the drive-through every 18 seconds, one mistake in every 3,600 orders (the industry average is one in 15), customer satisfaction scores of 98%, and health inspection scores above 97%. Turnover at the assistant manager level is under 2%, and in three decades Pal's has lost only seven general managers—two of them to retirement. Annual turnover on the front lines is about 34%—half the industry average. Pal's trains its employees extensively: New frontline workers receive 135 hours of instruction, on average (the industry average is about two hours). As a result, employees are confident that they can solve problems on their own and can stop processes if something does not seem right. (They also know they can ask for help.) When I was conducting interviews for a case on Pal's, a general manager gave me an example of how he encourages frontline workers to make decisions themselves: "A 16-year-old [employee] shows me a hot dog bun with flour on it and asks me if it's OK. My response: 'Your call. Would you sell it?'"

Let employees define their missions. Morning Star, a California-based tomato processing company, has employees write "personal commercial mission statements" that reflect who they are and specify their goals for a given time period, ones that will contribute to the company's success. The statements are embedded in contracts known as "colleague letters of understanding," or CLOUs, which employees negotiate with coworkers, each spelling out how he or she will collaborate with others. The personal commercial mission of Morning Star's founder, Chris Rufer, is "to advance tomato technology to be the best in the world and operate these factories so they are pristine." That of one sales and marketing employee is "to indelibly mark 'Morning Star Tomato Products' on the tongue and brain of every commercial tomato product user." That of one employee in the shipping unit is "to reliably and efficiently provide our customers with marvelously attractive loads of desired product."

Step 2: Encourage Employees to Bring Out Their Signature Strengths

Michelangelo described sculpting as a process whereby the artist releases an ideal figure from the block of stone in which it slumbers. We all possess ideal forms, the signature strengths—being social connectors, for example, or being able to see the positive in any situation—that we use naturally in our lives. And we all have a drive to do what we do best and be recognized accordingly. A leader's task is to encourage employees to sculpt their jobs to bring out their strengths—and to sculpt his or her own job, too. The actions below can help.

Give employees opportunities to identify their strengths. In a research project I conducted with Dan Cable, Brad Staats, and the University of Michigan's Julia Lee, leaders of national and local government agencies across the globe reflected each morning on their signature strengths and how to use them. They also read descriptions of times when they were at their best, written by people in their personal and professional networks. These leaders displayed more engagement and innovative behavior than members of a control group, and their teams performed better.

Tailor jobs to employees' strengths. Facebook is known for hiring smart people regardless of the positions currently open in the company, gathering information about their strengths, and designing their jobs accordingly. Another example is Osteria Francescana, a Michelin three-star restaurant in Modena, Italy, that won first place in the 2016 World's 50 Best Restaurant awards. Most restaurants, especially top-ranked ones, observe a strict hierarchy, with specific titles for each position. But at Osteria Francescana, jobs and their attendant responsibilities are tailored to individual workers.

Discovering employees' strengths takes time and effort. Massimo Bottura, the owner and head chef, rotates interns through various positions for at least a few months so that he and his team can configure jobs to play to the newcomers' strengths. This ensures that employees land where they fit best.

If such a process is too ambitious for your organization, consider giving employees some freedom to choose responsibilities within their assigned roles.

Step 3: Question the Status Quo, and Encourage Employees to Do the Same

Although businesses can benefit from repeatable practices that ensure consistency, they can also stimulate employee engagement and innovation by questioning standard procedures—"the way we've always done it." Here are some proven tactics.

Ask "Why?" and "What if?" By regularly asking employees such questions, Max Zanardi, for several years the general manager of the Ritz-Carlton in Istanbul, creatively led them to redefine luxury by providing customers with authentic and unusual experiences. For example, employees had traditionally planted flowers each year on the terrace outside the hotel's restaurant. One day Zanardi asked, "Why do we always plant flowers? How about vegetables? What about herbs?" This resulted in a terrace garden featuring herbs and heirloom tomatoes used in the restaurant—things guests very much appreciated.

Leaders who question the status quo give employees reasons to stay engaged and often spark fresh ideas that can rejuvenate the business.

Stress that the company is not perfect. Ed Catmull, the cofounder and president of Pixar Animation Studios, worried that new hires would be too awed by Pixar's success to challenge existing practices (see "How Pixar Fosters Collective Creativity," HBR, September 2008). So during onboarding sessions, his speeches included examples of the company's mistakes. Emphasizing that we are all human and that the organization will never be perfect gives employees freedom to engage in constructive nonconformity.

Excel at the basics. Ensuring that employees have deep knowledge about the way things usually operate provides them with a foundation for constructively questioning the status quo. This philosophy underlies the many hours Pal's devotes to training: Company leaders want employees to be expert in all aspects of their work. Similarly, Bottura believes that to create innovative dishes, his chefs must be well versed in classic cooking techniques.

Step 4: Create Challenging Experiences

It's easy for workers to get bored and fall back on routine when their jobs involve little variety or challenge. And employees who find their work boring lack the motivation to perform well and creatively, whereas work that is challenging enhances their engagement. Research led by David H. Zald, of Vanderbilt University, shows that novel behavior, such as trying something new or risky, triggers the release of dopamine, a chemical that helps keep us motivated and eager to innovate.

Leaders can draw on the following tactics when structuring employees' jobs:

Maximize variety. This makes it less likely that employees will go on autopilot and more likely that they will come up with innovative ways to improve what they're doing. It also boosts performance, as Brad Staats and I found in our analysis of two and a half years' worth of transaction data from a Japanese bank department responsible for processing home loan applications. The mortgage line involved 17 distinct tasks, including scanning applications, comparing scanned documents to originals, entering application data into the computer system, assessing whether information complied with underwriting standards, and conducting credit checks. Workers who were assigned diverse tasks from day to day were more productive than others (as measured by the time taken to complete each task); the variety kept them motivated. This allowed the bank to process applications more quickly, increasing its competitiveness.

Variety can be ensured in a number of ways. Pal's rotates employees through tasks (taking orders, grilling, working the register, and so on) in a different order each day. Some companies forgo defined career trajectories and instead move employees through various positions within departments or teams over the course of months or years.

In addition to improving engagement, job rotation broadens individuals' skill sets, creating a more flexible workforce. This makes it easier to find substitutes if someone falls ill or abruptly quits and to shift people from tasks where they are no longer needed (see "Why 'Good Jobs' Are Good for Retailers," HBR, January–February 2012).

Continually inject novelty into work. Novelty is a powerful force. When something new happens at work, we pay attention, engage, and tend to remember it. We are less likely to take our work for granted when it continues to generate strong feelings. Novelty in one's job is more satisfying than stability.

So, how can leaders inject it into work? Bottura throws last-minute menu changes at his team to keep excitement high. At Pal's, employees learn the order of their tasks for the day only when they get to work.

Leaders can also introduce novelty by making sure that projects include a few people who are somewhat out of their comfort zone, or by periodically giving teams new challenges (for instance, asking them to deliver a product faster than in the past). They can assign employees to teams charged with designing a new work process or piloting a new service.

Identify opportunities for personal learning and growth. Giving people such experiences is an essential way to promote constructive nonconformity, research has shown. For instance, in a field study conducted at a global consulting firm, colleagues and I found that when onboarding didn't just focus on performance but also spotlighted opportunities for learning and growth, engagement and innovative behaviors were higher six months later. Companies often identify growth opportunities during performance reviews, of course, but there are many other ways to do so. Chefs at Osteria Francescana can accompany Bottura to cooking events that expose them to other countries, cuisines, traditions, arts, and culture—all potential sources of inspiration for new dishes. When I worked as a research consultant at Disney, in the summer of 2010, I learned that members of the Imagineering R&D group were encouraged to belong to professional societies, attend conferences, and publish in academic and professional journals. Companies can help pay for courses that may not strictly relate to employees' current jobs but would nonetheless expand their skill sets or fuel their curiosity.

Give employees responsibility and accountability. At Morning Star, if employees need new equipment to do their work—even something that costs thousands of dollars—they may buy it. If they see a process that would benefit from different skills, they may hire someone. They must consult colleagues who would be affected (other people who would use the equipment, say), but they don't need approval from above. Because there are no job titles at Morning Star, how employees influence others—and thus get work done—is determined mainly by how their colleagues perceive the quality of their decisions.

Step 5: Foster Broader Perspectives

We often focus so narrowly on our own point of view that we have trouble understanding others' experiences and perspectives. And as we assume high-level positions, research shows, our egocentric focus becomes stronger. Here are some ways to combat it:

Create opportunities for employees to view problems from multiple angles. We all tend to be self-serving in terms of how we process information and generate (or fail to generate) alternatives to the status quo. Leaders can help employees overcome this tendency by encouraging them to view problems from different perspectives. At the electronics manufacturer Sharp, an oft-repeated maxim is "Be dragonflies, not flatfish." Dragonflies have compound eyes that can take in multiple perspectives at once; flatfish have both eyes on the same side of the head and can see in only one direction at a time.

Jon Olinto and Anthony Ackil, the founders of the fast-casual restaurant chain b.good, require all employees (including managers) and franchisees to be trained in every job—from prep to grill to register. (Unlike Pal's, however, b.good does not rotate people through jobs each day.) Being exposed to different perspectives increases engagement and innovative behaviors, research has found.

Use language that reduces self-serving bias. To prevent their traders from letting success go to their heads when the market is booming, some Wall Street firms regularly remind them, "Don't confuse brains with a bull market." At GE, terms such as "planting seeds" (to describe making investments that will produce fruitful results even after the managers behind them have moved on to other jobs) have entered the lexicon (see "How GE Teaches Teams to Lead Change," HBR, January 2009).

Hire people with diverse perspectives. Decades' worth of research has found that working among people from a variety of cultures and backgrounds helps us see problems in new ways and consider ideas that might otherwise go unnoticed, and it fosters the kind of creativity that champions change. At Osteria Francescana the two sous-chefs are Kondo "Taka" Takahiko, from Japan, and Davide di-Fabio, from Italy. They differ not only in country of origin but also in strengths and ways of thinking: Davide is comfortable with improvisation, for example, while Taka is obsessed with precision. Diversity in ways of thinking is a quality sought by Rachael Chong, the founder and CEO of the startup Catchafire. When interviewing job candidates, she describes potential challenges and carefully listens to see whether people come up with many possible solutions or get stuck on a single one. To promote innovation and new approaches, Ed Catmull hires prominent outsiders, gives them important roles, and publicly acclaims their contributions. But many organizations do just the opposite: hire people whose thinking mirrors that of the current management team.

Step 6: Voice and Encourage Dissenting Views

We often seek out and fasten on information that confirms our beliefs. Yet data that is inconsistent with our views and may even generate negative feelings (such as a sense of failure) can provide opportunities to improve our organizations and ourselves. Leaders can use a number of tactics to push employees out of their comfort zones.

Look for disconfirming evidence. Leaders shouldn't ask, "Who agrees with this course of action?" or "What information supports this view?" Instead they should ask, "What information suggests this might not be the right path to take?" Mellody Hobson, the president of Ariel Investments and the chair of the board of directors of DreamWorks Animation, regularly opens team meetings by reminding attendees that they don't need to be right; they need to bring up information that can help the team make the right decisions, which happens when members voice their concerns and disagree. At the Chicago Board of Trade, in-house investigators scrutinize trades that may violate exchange rules. To avoid bias in collecting information, they have been trained to ask open-ended interview questions, not ones that can be answered with a simple yes or no. Leaders can use a similar approach when discussing decisions. They should also take care not to depend on opinions but to assess whether the data supports or undermines the prevailing point of view.

Create dissent by default. Leaders can encourage debate during meetings by inviting individuals to take opposing points of view; they can also design processes to include dissent. When employees of Pal's suggest promising ideas for new menu items, the ideas are tested in three different stores: one whose owner-operator likes the idea ("the protagonist"), one whose owner-operator is skeptical ("the antagonist"), and one whose owner-operator has yet to form a strong opinion ("the neutral"). This ensures that dissenting views are aired and that they help inform the CEO's decisions about proposed items.

Identify courageous dissenters. Even if encouraged to push back, many timid or junior people won't. So make sure the team includes people you know will voice their concerns, writes Diana McLain Smith in *The Elephant in the Room: How Relationships Make or Break the Success of Leaders and Organizations*. Once the more reluctant employees see that opposing views are welcome, they will start to feel comfortable dissenting as well.

Striking the Right Balance

By adopting the strategies above, leaders can fight their own and their employees' tendency to conform when that would hurt the company's interests. But to strike the optimal balance between conformity and nonconformity, they must think carefully about the

Assessment: Are You a "Constructive Nonconformist"?

Find out how much of a rebel worker you are.

For decades, prevailing management wisdom has encouraged leaders to focus on designing efficient processes and getting employees to follow them. But conformity can hurt businesses. Innovation and high performance often result from behaviors that defy organizational norms—established ways of thinking and of doing things. How much does your company pressure you to conform? And are you succumbing to the pressure and hurting your chances of success? Take the following assessment (adapted from my ongoing research) to discover whether you're engaging in what I call constructive non-conformity: deviant behavior that benefits the organization.

When answering these questions, focus on the past month.	Never	Almost never	Some-times	Fairly often	Very often	Always
1. In the past month, how often have you refrained from opposing your team members just to avoid rocking the boat?	0	1	2	3	4	5
2. How often have you publicly supported ideas you privately disagreed with?	0	1	2	3	4	5
3. How often have you followed established rules or procedures, even though you suspected there was a better way to do things?	0	1	2	3	4	5
4. How often have you raised questions about the effectiveness of current processes or systems?	5	4	3	2	1	0
5. How often have you seen senior leaders challenge the status quo or ask employees to think outside the box?	5	4	3	2	1	0
6. How often have you felt pressured to conform to the cultural norms of your organization (how to dress, how to interact with others, how to do your work, and so on)?	0	1	2	3	4	5

When answering these questions, focus on the past month.	Never	Almost never	Some-times	Fairly often	Very often	Always
7. How often have you felt free to be yourself—to behave and express yourself in an authentic way?	5	4	3	2	1	0
8. How often have you been encouraged to solve problems on your own, without involving a supervisor?	5	4	3	2	1	0
9. How often has your job played to your strengths?	5	4	3	2	1	0
10. How often have you been challenged—urged to develop a new skill or to take on a task that pushed you out of your comfort zone?	5	4	3	2	1	0
11. How often have you sought information that was inconsistent with your views and might even prove you wrong?	5	4	3	2	1	0
12. How often have you and your team been encouraged to debate ideas or consider multiple perspectives before reaching a decision?	5	4	3	2	1	0

Score: 0–24 You're lucky: Your low score indicates that you are probably very engaged in your work, are performing at a high level, and are innovating frequently. Just make sure that you don't become complacent—the pressure to conform affects everyone. Keep being the rebel that you are!

Score: 25–30 Your score is average—and in this case, average is good. Scores in this range indicate that your ability to express yourself at work is at a healthy level, allowing you to be productive and innovative. To stay in this sweet spot, watch out for situations in which you feel pressured to conform.

Score: 31–39 Your higher-than-average score indicates a level of pressure that may be detrimental to your performance and your ability to innovate. You may also be disengaged. Try shaping your job in ways that allow you to be yourself and that bring out your talents and skills. Even small changes can let your authentic self shine through.

Score: 40–60 Your high score indicates an unproductive level of conformity. You're probably disengaged, and you're almost certainly having a hard time being your true self at work. It's critical that you find ways (big and small) to lower the pressure to conform, and that starts with allowing your authentic self to shine through. Act more like a rebel, and you and your organization will benefit.

boundaries within which employees will be free to deviate from the status quo. For instance, the way a manager leads her team can be up to her as long as her behavior is aligned with the company's purpose and values and she delivers on that purpose.

Morning Star's colleague letters of understanding provide such boundaries. They clearly state employees' goals and their responsibility to deliver on the organization's purpose but leave it up to individual workers to decide how to achieve those goals. Colleagues with whom an employee has negotiated a CLOU will let him know if his actions cross a line.

Brazil's Semco Group, a 3,000-employee conglomerate, similarly relies on peer pressure and other mechanisms to give employees considerable freedom while making sure they don't go overboard. The company has no job titles, dress code, or organizational charts. If you need a workspace, you reserve it in one of a few satellite offices scattered around São Paulo. Employees, including factory workers, set their own schedules and production quotas. They even choose the amount and form of their compensation. What prevents employees from taking advantage of this freedom? First, the company believes in transparency: All its financial information is public, so everyone knows what everyone else makes. People who pay themselves too much have to work with resentful colleagues. Second, employee compensation is tied directly to company profits, creating enormous peer pressure to keep budgets in line.

Ritz-Carlton, too, excels in balancing conformity and nonconformity. It depends on 3,000 standards developed over the years to ensure a consistent customer experience at all its hotels. These range from how to slice a lime to which toiletries to stock in the bathrooms. But employees have considerable freedom within those standards and can question them if they see ways to provide an even better customer experience. For instance, for many years the company has allowed staff members to spend up to $2,000 to address any customer complaint in the way they deem best. (Yes, that is $2,000 per employee per guest.) The hotel believes that business is most successful when employees have well-defined standards, understand the reasoning behind them, and are given autonomy in carrying them out.

Organizations, like individuals, can easily become complacent, especially when business is going well. Complacency often sets in because of too much conformity—stemming from peer pressure, acceptance of the status quo, and the interpretation of information in self-serving ways. The result is a workforce of people who feel they can't be themselves on the job, are bored, and don't consider others' points of view.

Constructive nonconformity can help companies avoid these problems. If leaders were to put just half the time they spend ensuring conformity into designing and installing mechanisms to encourage constructive deviance, employee engagement, productivity, and innovation would soar.

Further Reading

IN THE COURSE OF DEVELOPING this Big Idea on Rebel Talent, HBR asked Francesca Gino to provide a portfolio of content that could further inspire, advise, and help develop your understanding of the topic. Gino's curated list of materials on rebel talent runs the gamut from classic HBR articles to novels and more.

HBR Articles

While studying leaders and organizations that attract, develop, and manage talent so as to spark engagement and creativity, I found many insights in the pages of HBR.

- **"How Pixar Fosters Collective Creativity,"** Ed Catmull, September 2008
- **"Are You a High Potential?,"** Douglas A. Ready, Jay A. Conger, and Linda A. Hill, June 2010
- **"How to Hang On to Your High Potentials,"** Claudio Fernández-Aráoz, Boris Groysberg, and Nitin Nohria, October 2011
- **"How GE Teaches Teams to Lead Change,"** Steven Prokesch, January 2009
- **"Managing Without Managers,"** Ricardo Semler, September–October 1989
- **"Why My Former Employees Still Work for Me,"** Ricardo Semler, January–February 1994

Books

I've found inspiration in books from as far back as the 1950s that document how and why companies create pressure to conform and what can be done to combat it.

- *The Organization Man,* William H. Whyte, 1956
- *Reinventing Organizations: A Guide to Creating Organizations Inspired by the Next Stage of Human Consciousness,* Frederic Laloux, 2014
- *The Art of Being Unmistakable: A Collection of Essays About Making a Dent in the Universe,* Srinivas Rao, 2013
- *Bartleby, the Scrivener,* Herman Melville, 1853
- *Collective Genius: The Art and Practice of Leading Innovation,* Linda A. Hill, Greg Brandeau, Emily Truelove, and Kent Lineback, 2014

Case Studies

The best way to learn how to foster constructive nonconformity is to dig into how actual companies did so.

- *"Sun Hydraulics: Leading in Tough Times (A),"* Linda A. Hill and Jennifer M. Suesse, 2003
- *"Pal's Sudden Service—Scaling an Organizational Model to Drive Growth,"* Gary P. Pisano, Francesca Gino, and Bradley R. Staats, 2016
- *"The Morning Star Company: Self-Management at Work,"* Francesca Gino and Bradley R. Staats, 2013

Other Articles

- *"Monkeys Are Adept at Picking Up Social Cues, Research Shows,"* Pam Belluck, *New York Times,* 2013
- *"For Some Flight Attendants, Shtick Comes With the Safety Spiel,"* Zach Schonbrun, *New York Times,* 2016
- *"I'm Quite Eccentric Within Accepted Societal Norms,"* Martin Grossman, *The Onion,* 2007

Originally published in October–November 2016. Reprint H035GG

Why Diversity Programs Fail

by Frank Dobbin and Alexandra Kalev

BUSINESSES STARTED CARING A LOT more about diversity after a series of high-profile lawsuits rocked the financial industry. In the late 1990s and early 2000s, Morgan Stanley shelled out $54 million—and Smith Barney and Merrill Lynch more than $100 million each—to settle sex discrimination claims. In 2007, Morgan was back at the table, facing a new class action, which cost the company $46 million. In 2013, Bank of America Merrill Lynch settled a race discrimination suit for $160 million. Cases like these brought Merrill's total 15-year payout to nearly *half a billion* dollars.

It's no wonder that Wall Street firms now require new hires to sign arbitration contracts agreeing not to join class actions. They have also expanded training and other diversity programs. But on balance, equality isn't improving in financial services or elsewhere. Although the proportion of managers at U.S. commercial banks who were Hispanic rose from 4.7% in 2003 to 5.7% in 2014, white women's representation dropped from 39% to 35%, and black men's from 2.5% to 2.3%. The numbers were even worse in investment banks (though that industry is shrinking, which complicates the analysis). Among all U.S. companies with 100 or more employees, the proportion of black men in management increased just slightly—from 3% to 3.3%—from 1985 to 2014. White women saw bigger gains from 1985 to 2000—rising from 22% to 29% of managers—but their numbers haven't budged since then. Even in Silicon Valley, where many leaders tout the need to increase diversity for both business and social justice reasons, bread-and-butter tech jobs remain dominated by white men.

It shouldn't be surprising that most diversity programs aren't increasing diversity. Despite a few new bells and whistles, courtesy of big data, companies are basically doubling down on the same approaches they've used since the 1960s—which often make things worse, not better. Firms have long relied on diversity training to reduce bias on the job, hiring tests and performance ratings to limit it in recruitment and promotions, and grievance systems to give employees a way to challenge managers. Those tools are designed to preempt lawsuits by policing managers' thoughts and actions. Yet laboratory studies show that this kind of force-feeding can activate bias rather than stamp it out. As social scientists have found, people often rebel against rules to assert their autonomy. Try to coerce me to do X, Y, or Z, and I'll do the opposite just to prove that I'm my own person.

In analyzing three decades' worth of data from more than 800 U.S. firms and interviewing hundreds of line managers and executives at length, we've seen that companies get better results when they ease up on the control tactics. It's more effective to engage managers in solving the problem, increase their on-the-job contact with female and minority workers, and promote social accountability—the desire to look fair-minded. That's why interventions such as targeted college recruitment, mentoring programs, self-managed teams, and task forces have boosted diversity in businesses. Some of the most effective solutions aren't even designed with diversity in mind.

Here, we dig into the data, the interviews, and company examples to shed light on what doesn't work and what does.

Why You Can't Just Outlaw Bias

Executives favor a classic command-and-control approach to diversity because it boils expected behaviors down to dos and don'ts that are easy to understand and defend. Yet this approach also flies in the face of nearly everything we know about how to motivate people to

Idea in Brief

The Problem

To reduce bias and increase diversity, organizations are relying on the same programs they've been using since the 1960s. Some of these efforts make matters worse, not better.

The Reason

Most diversity programs focus on controlling managers' behavior, and as studies show, that approach tends to activate bias rather than quash it. People rebel against rules that threaten their autonomy.

The Solution

Instead of trying to police managers' decisions, the most effective programs engage people in working for diversity, increase their contact with women and minorities, and tap into their desire to look good to others.

make changes. Decades of social science research point to a simple truth: You won't get managers on board by blaming and shaming them with rules and reeducation. Let's look at how the most common top-down efforts typically go wrong.

Diversity training

Do people who undergo training usually shed their biases? Researchers have been examining that question since before World War II, in nearly a thousand studies. It turns out that while people are easily taught to respond correctly to a questionnaire about bias, they soon forget the right answers. The positive effects of diversity training rarely last beyond a day or two, and a number of studies suggest that it can activate bias or spark a backlash. Nonetheless, nearly half of midsize companies use it, as do nearly all the *Fortune* 500.

Many firms see adverse effects. One reason is that three-quarters use negative messages in their training. By headlining the legal case for diversity and trotting out stories of huge settlements, they issue an implied threat: "Discriminate, and the company will pay the price." We understand the temptation—that's how we got your attention in the first paragraph—but threats, or "negative incentives," don't win converts.

Another reason is that about three-quarters of firms with training still follow the dated advice of the late diversity guru R. Roosevelt

Thomas Jr. "If diversity management is strategic to the organization," he used to say, diversity training must be mandatory, and management has to make it clear that "if you can't deal with that, then we have to ask you to leave." But five years after instituting required training for managers, companies saw no improvement in the proportion of white women, black men, and Hispanics in management, and the share of black women actually decreased by 9%, on average, while the ranks of Asian-American men and women shrank by 4% to 5%. Trainers tell us that people often respond to compulsory courses with anger and resistance—and many participants actually report more animosity toward other groups afterward.

But voluntary training evokes the opposite response ("I chose to show up, so I must be pro-diversity"), leading to better results: increases of 9% to 13% in black men, Hispanic men, and Asian-American men and women in management five years out (with no decline in white or black women). Research from the University of Toronto reinforces our findings: In one study white subjects read a brochure critiquing prejudice toward blacks. When people felt pressure to agree with it, the reading strengthened their bias against blacks. When they felt the choice was theirs, the reading reduced bias.

Companies too often signal that training is remedial. The diversity manager at a national beverage company told us that the top brass uses it to deal with problem groups. "If there are a number of complaints . . . or, God forbid, some type of harassment case . . . leaders say, 'Everyone in the business unit will go through it again.'" Most companies with training have special programs for managers. To be sure, they're a high-risk group because they make the hiring, promotion, and pay decisions. But singling them out implies that they're the worst culprits. Managers tend to resent that implication and resist the message.

Hiring tests
Some 40% of companies now try to fight bias with mandatory hiring tests assessing the skills of candidates for frontline jobs. But managers don't like being told that they can't hire whomever they

please, and our research suggests that they often use the tests selectively. Back in the 1950s, following the postwar migration of blacks northward, Swift & Company, Chicago meatpackers, instituted tests for supervisor and quality-checking jobs. One study found managers telling blacks that they had failed the test and then promoting whites who hadn't been tested. A black machine operator reported: "I had four years at Englewood High School. I took an exam for a checker's job. The foreman told me I failed" and gave the job to a white man who "didn't take the exam."

This kind of thing still happens. When we interviewed the new HR director at a West Coast food company, he said he found that white managers were making only strangers—most of them minorities— take supervisor tests and hiring white friends without testing them. "If you are going to test one person for this particular job title," he told us, "you need to test everybody."

But even managers who test everyone applying for a position may ignore the results. Investment banks and consulting firms build tests into their job interviews, asking people to solve math and scenario-based problems on the spot. While studying this practice, Kellogg professor Lauren Rivera played a fly on the wall during hiring meetings at one firm. She found that the team paid little attention when white men blew the math test but close attention when women and blacks did. Because decision makers (deliberately or not) cherry-picked results, the testing amplified bias rather than quashed it.

Companies that institute written job tests for managers—about 10% have them today—see decreases of 4% to 10% in the share of managerial jobs held by white women, African-American men and women, Hispanic men and women, and Asian-American women over the next five years. There are significant declines among white and Asian-American women—groups with high levels of education, which typically score well on standard managerial tests. So group differences in test-taking skills don't explain the pattern.

Performance ratings
More than 90% of midsize and large companies use annual performance ratings to ensure that managers make fair pay and promotion

decisions. Identifying and rewarding the best workers isn't the only goal—the ratings also provide a litigation shield. Companies sued for discrimination often claim that their performance rating systems prevent biased treatment.

But studies show that raters tend to lowball women and minorities in performance reviews. And some managers give everyone high marks to avoid hassles with employees or to keep their options open when handing out promotions. However managers work around performance systems, the bottom line is that ratings don't boost diversity. When companies introduce them, there's no effect on minority managers over the next five years, and the share of white women in management drops by 4%, on average.

Grievance procedures

This last tactic is meant to identify and rehabilitate biased managers. About half of midsize and large firms have systems through which employees can challenge pay, promotion, and termination decisions. But many managers—rather than change their own behavior or address discrimination by others—try to get even with or belittle employees who complain. Among the nearly 90,000 discrimination complaints made to the Equal Employment Opportunity Commission in 2015, 45% included a charge of retaliation—which suggests that the original report was met with ridicule, demotion, or worse.

Once people see that a grievance system isn't warding off bad behavior in their organization, they may become less likely to speak up. Indeed, employee surveys show that most people don't report discrimination. This leads to another unintended consequence: Managers who receive few complaints conclude that their firms don't have a problem. We see this a lot in our interviews. When we talked with the vice president of HR at an electronics firm, she mentioned the widely publicized "difficulties other corporations are having" and added, "We have not had any of those problems . . . we have gone almost four years without any kind of discrimination complaint!" What's more, lab studies show that protective measures like grievance systems lead people to drop their guard and let bias affect their decisions, because they think company policies will guarantee fairness.

Things don't get better when firms put in formal grievance systems; they get worse. Our quantitative analyses show that the managerial ranks of white women and all minority groups except Hispanic men decline—by 3% to 11%—in the five years after companies adopt them.

Still, most employers feel they need some sort of system to intercept complaints, if only because judges like them. One strategy that is gaining ground is the "flexible" complaint system, which offers not only a formal hearing process but also informal mediation. Since an informal resolution doesn't involve hauling the manager before a disciplinary body, it may reduce retaliation. As we'll show, making managers feel accountable without subjecting them to public rebuke tends to help.

Tools for Getting Managers on Board

If these popular solutions backfire, then what can employers do instead to promote diversity?

A number of companies have gotten consistently positive results with tactics that don't focus on control. They apply three basic principles: engage managers in solving the problem, expose them to people from different groups, and encourage social accountability for change.

Engagement

When someone's beliefs and behavior are out of sync, that person experiences what psychologists call "cognitive dissonance." Experiments show that people have a strong tendency to "correct" dissonance by changing either the beliefs or the behavior. So, if you prompt them to act in ways that support a particular view, their opinions shift toward that view. Ask them to write an essay defending the death penalty, and even the penalty's staunch opponents will come to see some merits. When managers actively help boost diversity in their companies, something similar happens: They begin to think of themselves as diversity champions.

Take *college recruitment programs* targeting women and minorities. Our interviews suggest that managers willingly participate when invited. That's partly because the message is positive: "Help us find a greater variety of promising employees!" And involvement is voluntary: Executives sometimes single out managers they think would be good recruiters, but they don't drag anyone along at gunpoint.

Managers who make college visits say they take their charge seriously. They are determined to come back with strong candidates from underrepresented groups—female engineers, for instance, or African-American management trainees. Cognitive dissonance soon kicks in—and managers who were wishy-washy about diversity become converts.

The effects are striking. Five years after a company implements a college recruitment program targeting female employees, the share of white women, black women, Hispanic women, and Asian-American women in its management rises by about 10%, on average. A program focused on minority recruitment increases the proportion of black male managers by 8% and black female managers by 9%.

Mentoring is another way to engage managers and chip away at their biases. In teaching their protégés the ropes and sponsoring them for key training and assignments, mentors help give their charges the breaks they need to develop and advance. The mentors then come to believe that their protégés merit these opportunities— whether they're white men, women, or minorities. That is cognitive dissonance—"Anyone I sponsor must be deserving"— at work again.

While white men tend to find mentors on their own, women and minorities more often need help from formal programs. One reason, as Georgetown's business school dean David Thomas discovered in his research on mentoring, is that white male executives don't feel comfortable reaching out informally to young women and minority men. Yet they are eager to mentor assigned protégés, and women and minorities are often first to sign up for mentors.

Mentoring programs make companies' managerial echelons significantly more diverse: On average they boost the representation of black, Hispanic, and Asian-American women, and Hispanic and Asian-American men, by 9% to 24%. In industries where plenty of college-educated nonmanagers are eligible to move up, like chemicals and electronics, mentoring programs also increase the ranks of white women and black men by 10% or more.

Only about 15% of firms have special college recruitment programs for women and minorities, and only 10% have mentoring programs. Once organizations try them out, though, the upside becomes clear. Consider how these programs helped Coca-Cola in the wake of a race discrimination suit settled in 2000 for a record $193 million. With guidance from a court-appointed external task force, executives in the North America group got involved in recruitment and mentoring initiatives for professionals and middle managers, working specifically toward measurable goals for minorities. Even top leaders helped to recruit and mentor, and talent-sourcing partners were required to broaden their recruitment efforts. After five years, according to former CEO and chairman Neville Isdell, 80% of all mentees had climbed at least one rung in management. Both individual and group mentoring were open to all races but attracted large numbers of African-Americans (who accounted for 36% of protégés). These changes brought important gains. From 2000 to 2006, African-Americans' representation among salaried employees grew from 19.7% to 23%, and Hispanics' from 5.5% to 6.4%. And while African-Americans and Hispanics respectively made up 12% and 4.9% of professionals and middle managers in 2002, just four years later those figures had risen to 15.5% and 5.9%.

This began a virtuous cycle. Today, Coke looks like a different company. This February, *Atlanta Tribune* magazine profiled 17 African-American women in VP roles and above at Coke, including CFO Kathy Waller.

Contact

Evidence that contact between groups can lessen bias first came to light in an unplanned experiment on the European front during World War II. The U.S. army was still segregated, and only whites served in combat roles. High casualties left General Dwight Eisenhower understaffed, and he asked for black volunteers for combat duty. When Harvard sociologist Samuel Stouffer, on leave at the War Department, surveyed troops on their racial attitudes, he found that whites whose companies had been joined by black platoons showed dramatically lower racial animus and greater willingness to work alongside blacks than those whose companies remained segregated.

Stouffer concluded that whites fighting alongside blacks came to see them as soldiers like themselves first and foremost. The key, for Stouffer, was that whites and blacks had to be working toward a common goal *as equals*—hundreds of years of close contact during and after slavery hadn't dampened bias.

Business practices that generate this kind of contact across groups yield similar results. Take *self-managed teams,* which allow people in different roles and functions to work together on projects as equals. Such teams increase contact among diverse types of people, because specialties within firms are still largely divided along racial, ethnic, and gender lines. For example, women are more likely than men to work in sales, whereas white men are more likely to be in tech jobs and management, and black and Hispanic men are more likely to be in production.

As in Stouffer's combat study, working side-by-side breaks down stereotypes, which leads to more equitable hiring and promotion. At firms that create self-managed work teams, the share of white women, black men and women, and Asian-American women in management rises by 3% to 6% over five years.

Rotating management trainees through departments is another way to increase contact. Typically, this kind of *cross-training* allows people to try their hand at various jobs and deepen their understanding of the whole organization. But it also has a positive impact on diversity, because it exposes both department heads and trainees to a wider variety of people. The result, we've seen, is a bump of 3% to 7% in white women, black men and women, and Asian-American men and women in management.

About a third of U.S. firms have self-managed teams for core operations, and nearly four-fifths use cross-training, so these tools are already available in many organizations. Though college recruitment and mentoring have a bigger impact on diversity—perhaps because they activate engagement in the diversity mission *and* create intergroup contact—every bit helps. Self-managed teams and cross-training have had more positive effects than mandatory diversity training, performance evaluations, job testing, or grievance procedures, which are supposed to promote diversity.

Social accountability

The third tactic, encouraging social accountability, plays on our need to look good in the eyes of those around us. It is nicely illustrated by an experiment conducted in Israel. Teachers in training graded identical compositions attributed to Jewish students with Ashkenazic names (European heritage) or with Sephardic names (African or Asian heritage). Sephardic students typically come from poorer families and do worse in school. On average, the teacher trainees gave the Ashkenazic essays Bs and the Sephardic essays Ds. The difference evaporated, however, when trainees were told that they would discuss their grades with peers. The idea that they might have to explain their decisions led them to judge the work by its quality.

In the workplace you'll see a similar effect. Consider this field study conducted by Emilio Castilla of MIT's Sloan School of Management: A firm found it consistently gave African-Americans smaller raises than whites, even when they had identical job titles and performance ratings. So Castilla suggested transparency to activate social accountability. The firm posted each unit's average performance rating and pay raise by race and gender. Once managers realized that employees, peers, and superiors would know which parts of the company favored whites, the gap in raises all but disappeared.

Corporate *diversity task forces* help promote social accountability. CEOs usually assemble these teams, inviting department heads to volunteer and including members of underrepresented groups. Every quarter or two, task forces look at diversity numbers for the whole company, for business units, and for departments to figure out what needs attention.

After investigating where the problems are—recruitment, career bottlenecks, and so on—task force members come up with solutions, which they then take back to their departments. They notice if their colleagues aren't volunteering to mentor or showing up at recruitment events. Accountability theory suggests that having a task force member in a department will cause managers in it to ask themselves, "Will this look right?" when making hiring and promotion decisions.

Which Diversity Efforts Actually Succeed?

IN 829 MIDSIZE AND LARGE U.S. FIRMS, we analyzed how various diversity initiatives affected the proportion of women and minorities in management. Here you can see which ones helped different groups gain ground—and which set them back, despite good intentions. (No bar means we can't say with statistical certainty if the program had any effect.)

Poor returns on the usual programs

The three most popular interventions made firms less diverse, not more, because managers resisted strong-arming.

% Change over five years

Mandatory diversity training for managers led to significant decreases for Asian-Americans and black women.

Testing job applicants hurt women and minorities—but not because they perform poorly. Hiring managers don't always test everyone (white men often get a pass) and don't interpret results consistently.

Grievance systems likewise reduced diversity pretty much across the board. Though they're meant to reform biased managers, they often lead to retaliation.

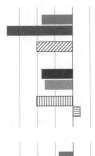

Legend:
- White men
- White women
- Black men
- Black women
- Hispanic men
- Hispanic women
- Asian men
- Asian women

Programs that get results

Companies do a better job of increasing diversity when they forgo the control tactics and frame their efforts more positively. The most effective programs spark engagement, increase contact among different groups, or draw on people's strong desire to

Voluntary training doesn't get managers' defenses up the way mandatory training does—and results in increases for several groups.

Self-managed teams aren't designed to improve diversity, but they help by increasing contact between groups, which are often concentrated in certain functions.

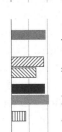

Cross-training also increases managers' exposure to people from different groups. Gains for some groups appear to come at a cost to Hispanic men.

College recruitment targeting women turns recruiting managers into diversity champions, so it also helps boost the numbers for black and Asian-American men.

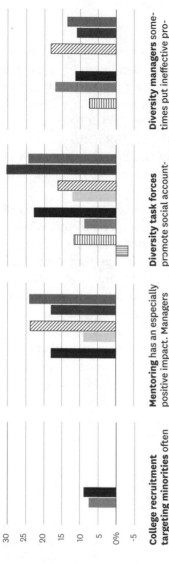

30
25
20
15
10
5
0%
-5

College recruitment targeting minorities often focuses on historically black schools, which lifts the numbers of African-American men and women.

Mentoring has an especially positive impact. Managers who sponsor women and minorities come to believe, through their increased contact, that their protégés deserve the training and opportunities they've received.

Diversity task forces promote social accountability because members bring solutions back to their departments—and notice whether their colleagues adopt them.

Diversity managers sometimes put ineffective programs in place but have a positive impact overall—in part because managers know someone might ask them about their hiring and promotion decisions.

Note: In our analysis, we've isolated the effects of diversity programs from everything else going on in the companies and in the economy.

Deloitte has seen how powerful social accountability can be. In 1992, Mike Cook, who was then the CEO, decided to try to stanch the hemorrhaging of female associates. Half the company's hires were women, but nearly all of them left before they were anywhere near making partner. As Douglas McCracken, CEO of Deloitte's consulting unit at the time, later recounted in HBR, Cook assembled a high-profile task force that "didn't immediately launch a slew of new organizational policies aimed at outlawing bad behavior" but, rather, relied on transparency to get results.

The task force got each office to monitor the career progress of its women and set its own goals to address local problems. When it became clear that the CEO and other managing partners were closely watching, McCracken wrote, "women started getting their share of premier client assignments and informal mentoring." And unit heads all over the country began getting questions from partners and associates about why things weren't changing faster. An external advisory council issued annual progress reports, and individual managers chose change metrics to add to their own performance ratings. In eight years turnover among women dropped to the same level as turnover among men, and the proportion of female partners increased from 5% to 14%—the highest percentage among the big accounting firms. By 2015, 21% of Deloitte's global partners were women, and in March of that year, Deloitte LLP appointed Cathy Engelbert as its CEO—making her the first woman to head a major accountancy.

Task forces are the trifecta of diversity programs. In addition to promoting accountability, they engage members who might have previously been cool to diversity projects and increase contact among the women, minorities, and white men who participate. They pay off, too: On average, companies that put in diversity task forces see 9% to 30% increases in the representation of white women and of each minority group in management over the next five years.

Diversity managers, too, boost inclusion by creating social accountability. To see why, let's go back to the finding of the teacher-in-training experiment, which is supported by many studies: When people know they *might* have to explain their decisions, they are less likely to act on bias. So simply having a diversity manager who could ask them questions prompts managers to step back and consider everyone who is qualified instead of hiring or promoting the first people who come to mind. Companies that appoint diversity managers see 7% to 18% increases in all underrepresented groups—except Hispanic men—in management in the following five years. Those are the gains after accounting for both effective and ineffective programs they put in place.

Only 20% of medium and large employers have task forces, and just 10% have diversity managers, despite the benefits of both. Diversity managers cost money, but task forces use existing workers, so they're a lot cheaper than some of the things that fail, such as mandatory training.

Leading companies like Bank of America Merrill Lynch, Facebook, and Google have placed big bets on accountability in the past couple of years. Expanding on Deloitte's early example, they're now posting complete diversity numbers for all to see. We should know in a few years if that moves the needle for them.

Strategies for controlling bias—which drive most diversity efforts—have failed spectacularly since they were introduced to promote equal opportunity. Black men have barely gained ground in corporate management since 1985. White women haven't progressed since 2000. It isn't that there aren't enough educated women and minorities out there—both groups have made huge educational gains over the past two generations. The problem is that we can't motivate people by forcing them to get with the program and punishing them if they don't.

The numbers sum it up. Your organization will become less diverse, not more, if you require managers to go to diversity training, try to regulate their hiring and promotion decisions, and put in a legalistic grievance system.

The very good news is that we know what does work—we just need to do more of it.

Originally published in July–August 2016. Reprint R1607C

What So Many People Don't Get About the U.S. Working Class

by Joan C. Williams

MY FATHER-IN-LAW GREW UP eating blood soup. He hated it, whether because of the taste or the humiliation, I never knew. His alcoholic father regularly drank up the family wage, and the family was often short on food money. They were evicted from apartment after apartment.

He dropped out of school in eighth grade to help support the family. Eventually he got a good, steady job he truly hated, as an inspector in a factory that made those machines that measure humidity levels in museums. He tried to open several businesses on the side but none worked, so he kept that job for 38 years. He rose from poverty to a middle-class life: the car, the house, two kids in Catholic school, the wife who worked only part-time. He worked incessantly. He had two jobs in addition to his full-time position, one doing yard work for a local magnate and another hauling trash to the dump.

Throughout the 1950s and 1960s, he read the *Wall Street Journal* and voted Republican. He was a man before his time: a blue-collar white man who thought the union was a bunch of jokers who took your money and never gave you anything in return. Starting in 1970, many blue-collar whites followed his example. This week, their candidate won the presidency.

For months, the only thing that's surprised me about Donald Trump is my friends' astonishment at his success. What's driving it is the class culture gap.

One little-known element of that gap is that the white working class (WWC) resents professionals but admires the rich. Class migrants (white-collar professionals born to blue-collar families) report that "professional people were generally suspect" and that managers are college kids "who don't know shit about how to do anything but are full of ideas about how I have to do my job," said Alfred Lubrano in *Limbo*. Barbara Ehrenreich recalled in 1990 that her blue-collar dad "could not say the word *doctor* without the virtual prefix *quack*. Lawyers were *shysters* . . . and professors were without exception *phonies*." Annette Lareau found tremendous resentment against teachers, who were perceived as condescending and unhelpful.

Michèle Lamont, in *The Dignity of Working Men,* also found resentment of professionals—but not of the rich. "[I] can't knock anyone for succeeding," a laborer told her. "There's a lot of people out there who are wealthy and I'm sure they worked darned hard for every cent they have," chimed in a receiving clerk. Why the difference? For one thing, most blue-collar workers have little direct contact with the rich outside of *Lifestyles of the Rich and Famous.* But professionals order them around every day. The dream is not to become upper-middle-class, with its different food, family, and friendship patterns; the dream is to live in your own class milieu, where you feel comfortable—just with more money. "The main thing is to be independent and give your own orders and not have to take them from anybody else," a machine operator told Lamont. Owning one's own business—that's the goal. That's another part of Trump's appeal.

Hillary Clinton, by contrast, epitomizes the dorky arrogance and smugness of the professional elite. The dorkiness: the pantsuits. The arrogance: the email server. The smugness: the basket of deplorables. Worse, her mere presence rubs it in that *even women* from her class can treat working-class men with disrespect. Look at how she condescends to Trump as unfit to hold the office of the presidency and dismisses his supporters as racist, sexist, homophobic, or xenophobic.

Trump's blunt talk taps into another blue-collar value: straight talk. "Directness is a working-class norm," notes Lubrano. As one blue-collar guy told him, "If you have a problem with me, come talk to me. If you have a way you want something done, come talk to me. I don't like people who play these two-faced games." Straight talk is seen as requiring manly courage, not being "a total wuss and a wimp," an electronics technician told Lamont. Of course Trump appeals. Clinton's clunky admission that she talks one way in public and another in private? Further proof she's a two-faced phony.

Manly dignity is a big deal for working-class men, and they're not feeling that they have it. Trump promises a world free of political correctness and a return to an earlier era, when men were men and women knew their place. It's comfort food for high-school-educated guys who could have been my father-in-law if they'd been born 30 years earlier. Today they feel like losers—or did until they met Trump.

Manly dignity is a big deal for most men. So is breadwinner status: Many still measure masculinity by the size of a paycheck. White working-class men's wages hit the skids in the 1970s and took another body blow during the Great Recession. Look, I wish manliness worked differently. But most men, like most women, seek to fulfill the ideals they've grown up with. For many blue-collar men, all they're asking for is basic human dignity (male varietal). Trump promises to deliver it.

The Democrats' solution? Last week the *New York Times* published an article advising men with high-school educations to take pink-collar jobs. Talk about insensitivity. Elite men, you will notice, are not flooding into traditionally feminine work. To recommend that for WWC men just fuels class anger.

Isn't what happened to Clinton unfair? Of course it is. It is unfair that she wasn't a plausible candidate until she was so overqualified she was suddenly unqualified due to past mistakes. It is unfair that Clinton is called a "nasty woman" while Trump is seen as a real man. It's unfair that Clinton only did so well in the first debate because she wrapped her candidacy in a shimmy of femininity. When she returned to attack mode, it was the right thing for a presidential candidate to do but the wrong thing for a woman to do. The election shows that sexism retains a deeper hold than most imagined. But women don't stand together: WWC women voted for Trump over Clinton by a whopping 28-point margin—62% to 34%. If they'd split 50-50, she would have won.

Class trumps gender, and it's driving American politics. Policy makers of both parties—but particularly Democrats if they are to regain their majorities—need to remember five major points.

Understand That Working Class Means Middle Class, Not Poor

The terminology here can be confusing. When progressives talk about the working class, typically they mean the poor. But the poor, in the bottom 30% of American families, are very different from Americans who are literally in the middle: the middle 50% of families whose median income was $64,000 in 2008. That is the true "middle class," and they call themselves either "middle class" or "working class."

"The thing that really gets me is that Democrats try to offer policies (paid sick leave! minimum wage!) that would *help* the working class," a friend just wrote me. A few days' paid leave ain't gonna support a family. Neither is minimum wage. WWC men aren't interested in working at McDonald's for $15 per hour instead of $9.50. What they want is what my father-in-law had: steady, stable, full-time jobs that deliver a solid middle-class life to the 75% of Americans who don't have a college degree. Trump promises that. I doubt he'll deliver, but at least he understands what they need.

Understand Working-Class Resentment of the Poor

Remember when President Obama sold Obamacare by pointing out that it delivered health care to 20 million people? Just another program that taxed the middle class to help the poor, said the WWC, and in some cases that's proved true: The poor got health insurance while some Americans just a notch richer saw their premiums rise.

Progressives have lavished attention on the poor for over a century. That (combined with other factors) led to social programs targeting them. Means-tested programs that help the poor but exclude the middle may keep costs and tax rates lower, but they are a recipe for class conflict. Example: 28.3% of poor families receive child-care subsidies, which are largely nonexistent for the middle class. So my sister-in-law worked full-time for Head Start, providing free child care for poor women while earning so little that she almost couldn't pay for her own. She resented this, especially the fact that some of the kids' moms did not work. One arrived late one day to pick up her child, carrying shopping bags from Macy's. My sister-in-law was livid.

J.D. Vance's much-heralded *Hillbilly Elegy* captures this resentment. Hard-living families like that of Vance's mother live alongside settled families like that of his biological father. While the hard-living succumb to despair, drugs, or alcohol, settled families keep to the straight and narrow, like my parents-in-law, who owned their home and sent both sons to college. To accomplish that, they lived a life of rigorous thrift and self-discipline. Vance's book passes harsh judgment on his hard-living relatives, which is not uncommon among settled families who kept their nose clean through sheer force of will. This is a second source of resentment against the poor.

Other books that get at this are *Hard Living on Clay Street* (1972) and *Working-Class Heroes* (2003).

Understand How Class Divisions Have Translated into Geography

The best advice I've seen so far for Democrats is the recommendation that hipsters move to Iowa. Class conflict now closely tracks the urban-rural divide. In the huge red plains between the thin blue coasts, shockingly high numbers of working-class men are unemployed or on disability, fueling a wave of despair deaths in the form of the opioid epidemic.

Vast rural areas are withering away, leaving trails of pain. When did you hear any American politician talk about that? Never.

Jennifer Sherman's *Those Who Work, Those Who Don't* (2009) covers this well.

If You Want to Connect with White Working-Class Voters, Place Economics at the Center

"The white working class is just so stupid. Don't they realize Republicans just use them every four years, and then screw them?" I have heard some version of this over and over again, and it's actually a sentiment the WWC agrees with, which is why they rejected the Republican establishment this year. But to them, the Democrats are no better.

Both parties have supported free-trade deals because of the net positive GDP gains, overlooking the blue-collar workers who lost work as jobs left for Mexico or Vietnam. These are precisely the voters in the crucial swing states of Ohio, Michigan, and Pennsylvania that Democrats have so long ignored. Excuse me. Who's stupid?

One key message is that trade deals are far more expensive than we've treated them, because sustained job development and training programs need to be counted as part of their costs.

At a deeper level, both parties need an economic program that can deliver middle-class jobs. Republicans have one: Unleash American business. Democrats? They remain obsessed with cultural issues. I fully understand why transgender bathrooms are important, but I also understand why progressives' obsession with prioritizing cultural issues infuriates many Americans whose chief concerns are economic.

Back when blue-collar voters used to be solidly Democratic (1930–1970), good jobs were at the core of the progressive agenda. A modern industrial policy would follow Germany's path. (Want really good scissors? Buy German.) Massive funding is needed for community college programs linked with local businesses to train workers for well-paying new economy jobs. Clinton mentioned this approach, along with 600,000 other policy suggestions. She did not stress it.

Avoid the Temptation to Write Off Blue-Collar Resentment as Racism

Economic resentment has fueled racial anxiety that, in some Trump supporters (and Trump himself), bleeds into open racism. But to write off WWC anger as nothing more than racism is intellectual comfort food, and it is dangerous.

National debates about policing are fueling class tensions today in precisely the same way they did in the 1970s, when college kids derided policemen as "pigs." This is a recipe for class conflict. Being in the police is one of the few good jobs open to Americans without a college education. Police get solid wages, great benefits, and a respected place in their communities. For elites to write them off as racists is a telling example of how, although race- and sex-based insults are no longer acceptable in polite society, class-based insults still are.

I do not defend police who kill citizens for selling cigarettes. But the current demonization of the police underestimates the difficulty of ending police violence against communities of color. Police need to make split-second decisions in life-threatening situations. I don't. If I had to, I might make some poor decisions too.

Saying this is so unpopular that I risk making myself a pariah among my friends on the left coast. But the biggest risk today for me and other Americans is continued class cluelessness. If we don't take steps to bridge the class culture gap, when Trump proves unable to bring steel back to Youngstown, Ohio, the consequences could turn dangerous.

In 2010, while on a book tour for *Reshaping the Work-Family Debate*, I gave a talk about all of this at the Harvard Kennedy School. The woman who ran the speaker series, a major Democratic operative, liked my talk. "You are saying exactly what the Democrats need to hear," she mused, "and they'll never listen." I hope now they will.

Originally published in November 2016. Reprint H03913

The Truth About Blockchain

by Marco Iansiti and Karim R. Lakhani

CONTRACTS, TRANSACTIONS, AND THE RECORDS of them are among the defining structures in our economic, legal, and political systems. They protect assets and set organizational boundaries. They establish and verify identities and chronicle events. They govern interactions among nations, organizations, communities, and individuals. They guide managerial and social action. And yet these critical tools and the bureaucracies formed to manage them have not kept up with the economy's digital transformation. They're like a rush-hour gridlock trapping a Formula 1 race car. In a digital world, the way we regulate and maintain administrative control has to change.

Blockchain promises to solve this problem. The technology at the heart of bitcoin and other virtual currencies, blockchain is an open, distributed ledger that can record transactions between two parties efficiently and in a verifiable and permanent way. The ledger itself can also be programmed to trigger transactions automatically. (See the sidebar "How Blockchain Works.")

With blockchain, we can imagine a world in which contracts are embedded in digital code and stored in transparent, shared databases, where they are protected from deletion, tampering, and revision. In this world every agreement, every process, every task, and every payment would have a digital record and signature that could be identified, validated, stored, and shared. Intermediaries

How Blockchain Works

Here are five basic principles underlying the technology.

1. **Distributed database.** Each party on a blockchain has access to the entire database and its complete history. No single party controls the data or the information. Every party can verify the records of its transaction partners directly, without an intermediary.

2. **Peer-to-peer transmission.** Communication occurs directly between peers instead of through a central node. Each node stores and forwards information to all other nodes.

3. **Transparency with pseudonymity.** Every transaction and its associated value are visible to anyone with access to the system. Each node, or user, on a blockchain has a unique 30-plus-character alphanumeric address that identifies it. Users can choose to remain anonymous or provide proof of their identity to others. Transactions occur between blockchain addresses.

4. **Irreversibility of records.** Once a transaction is entered in the database and the accounts are updated, the records cannot be altered, because they're linked to every transaction record that came before them (hence the term "chain"). Various computational algorithms and approaches are deployed to ensure that the recording on the database is permanent, chronologically ordered, and available to all others on the network.

5. **Computational logic.** The digital nature of the ledger means that blockchain transactions can be tied to computational logic and in essence programmed. So users can set up algorithms and rules that automatically trigger transactions between nodes.

---

like lawyers, brokers, and bankers might no longer be necessary. Individuals, organizations, machines, and algorithms would freely transact and interact with one another with little friction. This is the immense potential of blockchain.

Indeed, virtually everyone has heard the claim that blockchain will revolutionize business and redefine companies and economies. Although we share the enthusiasm for its potential, we worry about the hype. It's not just security issues (such as the 2014 collapse of one bitcoin exchange and the more recent hacks of others) that concern us. Our experience studying technological innovation tells us that if

Idea in Brief

The Hype

We've all heard that blockchain will revolutionize business, but it's going to take a lot longer than many people claim.

The Reason

Like TCP/IP (on which the internet was built), blockchain is a foundational technology that will require broad coordination. The level of complexity—technological, regulatory, and social—will be unprecedented.

The Truth

The adoption of TCP/IP suggests blockchain will follow a fairly predictable path. While the journey will take years, it's not too early for businesses to start planning.

there's to be a blockchain revolution, many barriers—technological, governance, organizational, and even societal—will have to fall. It would be a mistake to rush headlong into blockchain innovation without understanding how it is likely to take hold.

True blockchain-led transformation of business and government, we believe, is still many years away. That's because blockchain is not a "disruptive" technology, which can attack a traditional business model with a lower-cost solution and overtake incumbent firms quickly. Blockchain is a *foundational* technology: It has the potential to create new foundations for our economic and social systems. But while the impact will be enormous, it will take decades for blockchain to seep into our economic and social infrastructure. The process of adoption will be gradual and steady, not sudden, as waves of technological and institutional change gain momentum. That insight and its strategic implications are what we'll explore in this article.

Patterns of Technology Adoption

Before jumping into blockchain strategy and investment, let's reflect on what we know about technology adoption and, in particular, the transformation process typical of other foundational technologies. One of the most relevant examples is distributed computer networking technology, seen in the adoption of TCP/IP (transmission control protocol/internet protocol), which laid the groundwork for the development of the internet.

Introduced in 1972, TCP/IP first gained traction in a *single-use* case: as the basis for e-mail among the researchers on ARPAnet, the U.S. Department of Defense precursor to the commercial internet. Before TCP/IP, telecommunications architecture was based on "circuit switching," in which connections between two parties or machines had to be preestablished and sustained throughout an exchange. To ensure that any two nodes could communicate, telecom service providers and equipment manufacturers had invested billions in building dedicated lines.

TCP/IP turned that model on its head. The new protocol transmitted information by digitizing it and breaking it up into very small packets, each including address information. Once released into the network, the packets could take any route to the recipient. Smart sending and receiving nodes at the network's edges could disassemble and reassemble the packets and interpret the encoded data. There was no need for dedicated private lines or massive infrastructure. TCP/IP created an open, shared public network without any central authority or party responsible for its maintenance and improvement.

Traditional telecommunications and computing sectors looked on TCP/IP with skepticism. Few imagined that robust data, messaging, voice, and video connections could be established on the new architecture or that the associated system could be secure and scale up. But during the late 1980s and 1990s, a growing number of firms, such as Sun, NeXT, Hewlett-Packard, and Silicon Graphics, used TCP/IP, in part to create *localized* private networks within organizations. To do so, they developed building blocks and tools that broadened its use beyond e-mail, gradually replacing more-traditional local network technologies and standards. As organizations adopted these building blocks and tools, they saw dramatic gains in productivity.

TCP/IP burst into broad public use with the advent of the World Wide Web in the mid-1990s. New technology companies quickly emerged to provide the "plumbing"—the hardware, software, and services needed to connect to the now-public network and exchange information. Netscape commercialized browsers, web servers, and other tools and components that aided the development and adoption of internet services and applications. Sun drove the development of Java, the application-programming language. As information on the web grew exponentially, Infoseek, Excite, Alta-Vista, and Yahoo were born to guide users around it.

Once this basic infrastructure gained critical mass, a new generation of companies took advantage of low-cost connectivity by creating internet services that were compelling *substitutes* for existing businesses. CNET moved news online. Amazon offered more books for sale than any bookshop. Priceline and Expedia made it easier to buy airline tickets and brought unprecedented transparency to the process. The ability of these newcomers to get extensive reach at relatively low cost put significant pressure on traditional businesses like newspapers and brick-and-mortar retailers.

Relying on broad internet connectivity, the next wave of companies created novel, *transformative* applications that fundamentally changed the way businesses created and captured value. These companies were built on a new peer-to-peer architecture and generated value by coordinating distributed networks of users. Think of how eBay changed online retail through auctions, Napster changed the music industry, Skype changed telecommunications, and Google, which exploited user-generated links to provide more relevant results, changed web search.

Ultimately, it took more than 30 years for TCP/IP to move through all the phases—single use, localized use, substitution, and transformation—and reshape the economy. Today more than half the world's most valuable public companies have internet-driven, platform-based business models. The very foundations of our economy have changed. Physical scale and unique intellectual property no longer confer unbeatable advantages; increasingly, the economic leaders are enterprises that act as "keystones," proactively organizing, influencing, and coordinating widespread networks of communities, users, and organizations.

The New Architecture

Blockchain—a peer-to-peer network that sits on top of the internet—was introduced in October 2008 as part of a proposal for bitcoin, a virtual currency system that eschewed a central authority for issuing currency, transferring ownership, and confirming transactions. Bitcoin is the first application of blockchain technology.

The parallels between blockchain and TCP/IP are clear. Just as e-mail enabled bilateral messaging, bitcoin enables bilateral financial transactions. The development and maintenance of blockchain is open, distributed, and shared—just like TCP/IP's. A team of volunteers around the world maintains the core software. And just like e-mail, bitcoin first caught on with an enthusiastic but relatively small community.

TCP/IP unlocked new economic value by dramatically lowering the cost of connections. Similarly, blockchain could dramatically reduce the cost of transactions. It has the potential to become the system of record for all transactions. If that happens, the economy will once again undergo a radical shift, as new, blockchain-based sources of influence and control emerge.

Consider how business works now. Keeping ongoing records of transactions is a core function of any business. Those records track past actions and performance and guide planning for the future. They provide a view not only of how the organization works internally but also of the organization's outside relationships. Every organization keeps its own records, and they're private. Many organizations have no master ledger of all their activities; instead records are distributed across internal units and functions. The problem is, reconciling transactions across individual and private ledgers takes a lot of time and is prone to error.

For example, a typical stock transaction can be executed within microseconds, often without human intervention. However, the settlement—the ownership transfer of the stock—can take as long as a week. That's because the parties have no access to each other's ledgers and can't automatically verify that the assets are in fact owned and can be transferred. Instead a series of intermediaries act as guarantors of assets as the record of the transaction traverses organizations and the ledgers are individually updated.

In a blockchain system, the ledger is replicated in a large number of identical databases, each hosted and maintained by an interested party. When changes are entered in one copy, all the other copies are simultaneously updated. So as transactions occur, records of the value and assets exchanged are permanently entered in all ledgers. There is no need for third-party intermediaries to verify or transfer ownership. If a stock transaction took place on a blockchain-based system, it would be settled within seconds, securely and verifiably. (The infamous hacks that have hit bitcoin exchanges exposed weaknesses not in the blockchain itself but in separate systems linked to parties using the blockchain.)

A Framework for Blockchain Adoption

If bitcoin is like early e-mail, is blockchain decades from reaching its full potential? In our view the answer is a qualified yes. We can't predict exactly how many years the transformation will take, but we can guess which kinds of applications will gain traction first and how blockchain's broad acceptance will eventually come about.

In our analysis, history suggests that two dimensions affect how a foundational technology and its business use cases evolve. The first is novelty—the degree to which an application is new to the world. The more novel it is, the more effort will be required to ensure that users understand what problems it solves. The second dimension is complexity, represented by the level of ecosystem coordination involved—the number and diversity of parties that need to work together to produce value with the technology. For example, a social network with just one member is of little use; a social network is worthwhile only when many of your own connections have signed on to it. Other users of the application must be brought on board to generate value for all participants. The same will be true for many blockchain applications. And, as the scale and impact of those applications increase, their adoption will require significant institutional change.

How foundational technologies take hold

The adoption of foundational technologies typically happens in four phases. Each phase is defined by the novelty of the applications and the complexity of the coordination efforts needed to make them workable. Applications low in novelty and complexity gain acceptance first. Applications high in novelty and complexity take decades to evolve but can transform the economy. TCP/IP technology, introduced on ARPAnet in 1972, has already reached the transformation phase, but blockchain applications (in white) are in their early days.

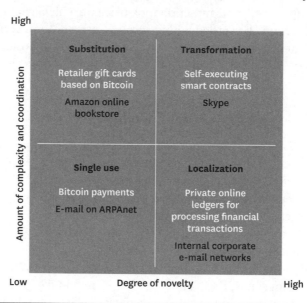

We've developed a framework that maps innovations against these two contextual dimensions, dividing them into quadrants. (See the exhibit "How foundational technologies take hold.") Each quadrant represents a stage of technology development. Identifying which one a blockchain innovation falls into will help executives understand the types of challenges it presents, the level of collaboration and consensus it needs, and the legislative and regulatory efforts it will require. The map will also suggest what kind of processes and infrastructure must be established to facilitate the innovation's adoption. Managers can use it to assess the state of blockchain development in any industry, as well as to evaluate strategic investments in their own blockchain capabilities.

Single use

In the first quadrant are low-novelty and low-coordination applications that create better, less costly, highly focused solutions. E-mail, a cheap alternative to phone calls, faxes, and snail mail, was a single-use application for TCP/IP (even though its value rose with the number of users). Bitcoin, too, falls into this quadrant. Even in its early days, bitcoin offered immediate value to the few people who used it simply as an alternative payment method. (You can think of it as a complex e-mail that transfers not just information but also actual value.) At the end of 2016 the value of bitcoin transactions was expected to hit $92 billion. That's still a rounding error compared with the $411 trillion in total global payments, but bitcoin is growing fast and increasingly important in contexts such as instant payments and foreign currency and asset trading, where the present financial system has limitations.

Localization

The second quadrant comprises innovations that are relatively high in novelty but need only a limited number of users to create immediate value, so it's still relatively easy to promote their adoption. If blockchain follows the path network technologies took in business, we can expect blockchain innovations to build on single-use applications to create local private networks on which multiple organizations are connected through a distributed ledger.

Much of the initial private blockchain-based development is taking place in the financial services sector, often within small networks of firms, so the coordination requirements are relatively modest. Nasdaq is working with Chain.com, one of many blockchain infrastructure providers, to offer technology for processing and validating financial transactions. Bank of America, JPMorgan, the New York Stock Exchange, Fidelity Investments, and Standard Chartered are testing blockchain technology as a replacement for paper-based and manual transaction processing in such areas as trade finance, foreign exchange, cross-border settlement, and securities settlement. The Bank of Canada is testing a digital currency called CAD-coin for interbank transfers. We anticipate a proliferation of private blockchains that serve specific purposes for various industries.

Substitution

The third quadrant contains applications that are relatively low in novelty because they build on existing single-use and localized applications, but are high in coordination needs because they involve broader and increasingly public uses. These innovations aim to replace entire ways of doing business. They face high barriers to adoption, however; not only do they require more coordination but the processes they hope to replace may be full-blown and deeply embedded within organizations and institutions. Examples of substitutes include cryptocurrencies—new, fully formed currency systems that have grown out of the simple bitcoin payment technology. The critical difference is that a cryptocurrency requires every party that does monetary transactions to adopt it, challenging governments and institutions that have long handled and overseen such transactions. Consumers also have to change their behavior and understand how to implement the new functional capability of the cryptocurrency.

A recent experiment at MIT highlights the challenges ahead for digital currency systems. In 2014 the MIT Bitcoin Club provided each of MIT's 4,494 undergraduates with $100 in bitcoin. Interestingly, 30% of the students did not even sign up for the free money, and 20% of the sign-ups converted the bitcoin to cash within a few weeks. Even the technically savvy had a tough time understanding how or where to use bitcoin.

One of the most ambitious substitute blockchain applications is Stellar, a nonprofit that aims to bring affordable financial services, including banking, micropayments, and remittances, to people who've never had access to them. Stellar offers its own virtual currency, lumens, and also allows users to retain on its system a range of assets, including other currencies, telephone minutes, and data credits. Stellar initially focused on Africa, particularly Nigeria, the largest economy there. It has seen significant adoption among its target population and proved its cost-effectiveness. But its future is by no means certain, because the ecosystem coordination challenges are high. Although grassroots adoption has demonstrated the viability of Stellar, to become a banking standard, it will need to influence government policy and persuade central banks and large organizations to use it. That could take years of concerted effort.

Transformation

Into the last quadrant fall completely novel applications that, if successful, could change the very nature of economic, social, and political systems. They involve coordinating the activity of many actors and gaining institutional agreement on standards and processes. Their adoption will require major social, legal, and political change.

"Smart contracts" may be the most transformative blockchain application at the moment. These automate payments and the transfer of currency or other assets as negotiated conditions are met. For example, a smart contract might send a payment to a supplier as soon as a shipment is delivered. A firm could signal via blockchain that a particular good has been received—or the product could have GPS functionality, which would automatically log a location update that, in turn, triggered a payment. We've already seen a few early experiments with such self-executing contracts in the areas of venture funding, banking, and digital rights management.

The implications are fascinating. Firms are built on contracts, from incorporation to buyer-supplier relationships to employee relations. If contracts are automated, then what will happen to traditional firm structures, processes, and intermediaries like lawyers and accountants? And what about managers? Their roles would all radically change. Before we get too excited here, though, let's remember that we are decades away from the widespread adoption of smart contracts. They cannot be effective, for instance, without institutional buy-in. A tremendous degree of coordination and clarity on how smart contracts are designed, verified, implemented, and enforced will be required. We believe the institutions responsible for those daunting tasks will take a long time to evolve. And the technology challenges—especially security—are daunting.

Guiding Your Approach to Blockchain Investment

How should executives think about blockchain for their own organizations? Our framework can help companies identify the right opportunities.

For most, the easiest place to start is single-use applications, which minimize risk because they aren't new and involve little coordination with third parties. One strategy is to add bitcoin as a payment mechanism. The infrastructure and market for bitcoin are already well developed, and adopting the virtual currency will force a variety of functions, including IT, finance, accounting, sales, and marketing, to build blockchain capabilities. Another low-risk approach is to use blockchain internally as a database for applications like managing physical and digital assets, recording internal transactions, and verifying identities. This may be an especially useful solution for companies struggling to reconcile multiple internal databases. Testing out single-use applications will help organizations develop the skills they need for more-advanced applications. And thanks to the emergence of cloud-based blockchain services from both start-ups and large platforms like Amazon and Microsoft, experimentation is getting easier all the time.

Localized applications are a natural next step for companies. We're seeing a lot of investment in private blockchain networks right now, and the projects involved seem poised for real short-term impact. Financial services companies, for example, are finding that the private blockchain networks they've set up with a limited number of trusted counterparties can significantly reduce transaction costs.

Organizations can also tackle specific problems in transactions across boundaries with localized applications. Companies are already using blockchain to track items through complex supply chains, for instance. This is happening in the diamond industry, where gems are being traced from mines to consumers. The technology for such experiments is now available off-the-shelf.

Developing substitute applications requires careful planning, since existing solutions may be difficult to dislodge. One way to go may be to focus on replacements that won't require end users to change their behavior much but present alternatives to expensive or unattractive solutions. To get traction, substitutes must deliver functionality as good as a traditional solution's and must be easy for the ecosystem to absorb and adopt. First Data's foray into blockchain-based gift cards is a good example of a well-considered substitute. Retailers that offer them to consumers can dramatically lower costs per transaction and enhance security by using blockchain to track the flows of currency within accounts—without relying on external payment processors. These new gift cards even allow transfers of balances and transaction capability between merchants via the common ledger.

Transformative applications are still far away. But it makes sense to evaluate their possibilities now and invest in developing technology that can enable them. They will be most powerful when tied to a new business model in which the logic of value creation and capture departs from existing approaches. Such business models are hard to adopt but can unlock future growth for companies.

Consider how law firms will have to change to make smart contracts viable. They'll need to develop new expertise in software and blockchain programming. They'll probably also have to rethink their hourly payment model and entertain the idea of charging transaction or hosting fees for contracts, to name just two possible approaches. Whatever tack they take, executives must be sure they understand and have tested the business model implications before making any switch.

Transformative scenarios will take off last, but they will also deliver enormous value. Two areas where they could have a profound impact: large-scale public identity systems for such functions as passport control, and algorithm-driven decision making in the prevention of money laundering and in complex financial transactions that involve many parties. We expect these applications won't reach broad adoption and critical mass for at least another decade and probably more.

Transformative applications will also give rise to new platform-level players that will coordinate and govern the new ecosystems. These will be the Googles and Facebooks of the next generation. It will require patience to realize such opportunities. Though it may be premature to start making significant investments in them now, developing the required foundations for them—tools and standards—is still worthwhile.

In addition to providing a good template for blockchain's adoption, TCP/IP has most likely smoothed the way for it. TCP/IP has become ubiquitous, and blockchain applications are being built on top of the digital data, communication, and computation infrastructure, which lowers the cost of experimentation and will allow new use cases to emerge rapidly.

With our framework, executives can figure out where to start building their organizational capabilities for blockchain today. They need to ensure that their staffs learn about blockchain, to develop company-specific applications across the quadrants we've identified, and to invest in blockchain infrastructure.

But given the time horizons, barriers to adoption, and sheer complexity involved in getting to TCP/IP levels of acceptance, executives should think carefully about the risks involved in experimenting with blockchain. Clearly, starting small is a good way to develop the know-how to think bigger. But the level of investment should depend on the context of the company and the industry. Financial services companies are already well down the road to blockchain adoption. Manufacturing is not.

No matter what the context, there's a strong possibility that blockchain will affect your business. The very big question is when.

Further Reading

TO LEARN MORE ABOUT technology adoption, go to these articles on HBR.org:

- **"Digital Ubiquity: How Connections, Sensors, and Data Are Revolutionizing Business,"** Marco Iansiti and Karim R. Lakhani

- **"Strategy as Ecology,"** Marco Iansiti and Roy Levien

- **"Right Tech, Wrong Time,"** Ron Adner and Rahul Kapoor

Originally published in January–February 2017. Reprint R1701J

The Edison of Medicine

by Steven Prokesch

ONE MORNING LAST YEAR, James Dahlman came to Bob Langer's office at MIT's Koch Institute for Integrative Cancer Research to say good-bye. He was meeting with Langer and Dan Anderson—his doctoral advisers. The 29-year-old was about to take up his first faculty position, in the biomedical engineering department at Georgia Tech, and he wanted their advice.

"Do something that's big," Langer told him. "Do something that really can change the world rather than something incremental."

These were not just inspirational words for a former student. They are the watchcry that has guided Langer, a chemical engineer and a pioneer in the fields of controlled-release drug delivery and tissue engineering, throughout his four-decade career at MIT. And they are part of the formula that has made Langer Lab one of the most productive research facilities in the world.

Academic, corporate, and government labs—indeed, anyone leading a group of highly talented people from disparate fields—could learn much from Langer's model. He has a five-pronged approach to accelerating the pace of discoveries and ensuring that they make it out of academia and into the real world as products. It includes a focus on high-impact ideas, a process for crossing the proverbial "valley of death" between research and commercial development, methods for facilitating multidisciplinary collaboration, ways to make the constant turnover of researchers and the limited duration of project funding a plus, and a leadership style that balances freedom and support.

The United States alone spends roughly $500 billion a year on research, but "much of that is mundane," says H. Kent Bowen, an emeritus professor at Harvard Business School who has spent years studying academic and corporate labs. "If there were more highly collaborative, Langer-like labs that focused on high-impact research, the United States would realize its enormous potential for creating wealth."

Langer's achievements are remarkable on several counts. His h-index score, a measure of the number of a scholar's published papers and how often they have been cited, is 230—the highest of any engineer ever. His more than 1,100 current and pending patents have been licensed or sublicensed to some 300 pharmaceutical, chemical, biotechnology, and medical device companies, earning him the nickname "the Edison of medicine." Alone or in collaboration, his lab has given rise to 40 companies, all but one of which are still in existence, either as independent entities or as part of acquiring companies. Collectively, they have an estimated market value of more than $23 billion—excluding Living Proof, a hair products company that Unilever is acquiring for an undisclosed sum.

A final "product" of the lab is people: Scores of the roughly 900 researchers who have earned graduate degrees or worked as postdocs at the lab have gone on to distinguished careers in academia, business, and venture capital. Fourteen have been inducted into the National Academy of Engineering, 12 into the National Academy of Medicine.

The multidisciplinary approach is still a work in progress in academia, but it has been gathering steam there over the past decade or so, reflecting universities' growing interest in tackling real-world problems and spawning new businesses and a recognition that doing so often takes diverse expertise. Although it has long been common in the business world, companies too could improve their results by applying elements of Langer's research-to-product process, thereby creating brand-new offerings and refreshing or reinventing their businesses again and again.

Idea in Brief

The Problem

Early-stage research is expensive, risky, and unpredictable—so corporations shy away from it, leaving many opportunities unexplored.

The Solution

By pursuing research aimed at solving society's major problems, companies can make the world a better place *and* make lots of money.

The Model

MIT's Bob Langer has a proven formula for accelerating the pace of discoveries and getting them into the world as products—and it's one that any organization can draw on.

Focus on High-Impact Problems

One of Langer's mantras when choosing projects is: Consider the potential impact on society, not the money. The idea is that if you create something that makes a major difference, the customers and the money will come. It's a profound departure from the approach of many big companies: If an idea for a product is so radically new that discounted cash flow can't be calculated, they often won't pursue it, or they give up when the research hits an obstacle—as ambitious research almost always does.

To Langer, "impact" means the number of people an invention could help. The life sciences enterprises that have emerged from his lab have the potential to touch nearly 4.7 billion lives, according to Polaris Partners, a venture capital firm that has financed many of them. For example, one of the lab's products, on the market since 1996, is a wafer that can be implanted in the brain to deliver chemotherapy directly to the site of a glioblastoma. Another, recently handed over to a new company—Sigilon, based in Cambridge, Massachusetts—is a potential cure for type 1 diabetes, developed in concert with researchers at other universities: Encasing beta cells in a polymer, the researchers have shown, can protect them from the body's immune system yet allow them to detect the level of sugar in the blood and release the appropriate amounts of insulin.

With such concrete, ambitious projects on the lab's docket, the customers have indeed come: foundations, companies, scientists in other labs, and government agencies including the National Institutes of Health. Foundations and companies currently fund 63% of the lab's $17.3 million annual budget; they range from the Bill & Melinda Gates Foundation and the Prostate Cancer Foundation to Novo Nordisk and Hoffmann-La Roche. "A key reason we decided to work with Bob was his lab's track record in controlled delivery," says Dan Hartman, the director of integrated development and malaria at the Gates Foundation and the chief liaison between the foundation and the lab. "Bob and his team's creativity and technical expertise cannot be overemphasized."

A second criterion for project selection is fit with the lab's core areas: drug delivery, drug development, tissue engineering, and biomaterials. "Most of what we do is at the interface of materials, biology, and medicine," Langer says.

Third, he asks whether it's realistic to believe that the medical and scientific challenges can be met by applying or expanding existing science, either at his lab alone or in collaboration with others.

This approach defies a long-prevailing view about the research-to-product process—that it is linear and looks like this: *Basic research* (endeavors aimed at expanding knowledge of nature, without thought of practical use) leads to *applied,* or *translational, research* (efforts to solve practical problems), which in turn leads to *commercial development* (turning discoveries into actual processes and products)—all culminating in a *scale-up* to mass production. The paradigm can be traced to Vannevar Bush, the head of the National Defense Research Committee and the U.S. Office of Scientific Research and Development during World War II and a leading proponent of strong government support for basic scientific research.

Since the war, universities have conducted the lion's share of basic research, but corporations have participated too: Think of AT&T, Corning, DuPont, and IBM, to name just a few. In recent decades, though, big companies have come to see it as too expensive and risky: Results are slow and unpredictable, and capturing their value can be difficult. So they have increasingly turned to academia, sometimes buying or licensing discoveries or investing in or acquiring start-ups that develop them, other times funding academic research or having their scientists in academic labs.

However, the linear paradigm was never universally true. From the mid 19th century onward, great researchers have pushed the frontiers of basic science precisely to solve pressing societal problems. The Princeton political scientist Donald E. Stokes coined a term for the space in which they work: *Pasteur's quadrant,* reflecting Louis Pasteur's pursuit of a fundamental understanding of microbiology in order to combat disease and food spoilage. Other examples include Bell Labs, whose scientists made basic discoveries while improving and extending communications systems, and the U.S. Defense Advanced Research Projects Agency, or DARPA—one of the most successful innovation organizations ever.

Langer Lab resides in Pasteur's quadrant too. Although its researchers devote the bulk of their efforts to applied science and engineering that could solve critical problems, in the process they often push the boundaries of basic science. For example, one of Langer's most important discoveries was a way to release large-molecule drugs in the body via porous polymers at designated doses and times over several years. This involved expanding an area of physics and math known as percolation theory.

With some notable exceptions—Corning's efforts in quantum communications and materials for capturing carbon dioxide, IBM's in cognitive computing and smart cities, Alphabet's in health care and self-driving vehicles—firms today aren't striving to connect early-stage research with major real-world applications. "It's very rare, but I don't think it needs to be," says Gary P. Pisano, a professor at Harvard Business School. "If you solve some of society's big problems, you'll actually make a lot of money."

Susan Hockfield, a professor of neuroscience at the Koch Institute and a former president of MIT, agrees. "There's a lot of appropriate concern and skepticism about the state of corporate R&D," she says. "For example, pharma corporate R&D invests significantly in very early stage, exploratory research. Couldn't they be doing better if they partnered more effectively with nonindustry biologists and engineers? And I just finished service on a commission to review the national labs. I'm astonished by what a brilliant idea they are and by the high quality of their research, but could they be turning more of their discoveries into products for the marketplace?"

How to Innovate Like Langer

CORPORATIONS TYPICALLY SHY AWAY from early-stage research because it is expensive, risky, and unpredictable, making it difficult for the organization conducting it to capture the benefits. They could revitalize their research operations by taking an alternative approach and adopting some or all of the following principles from Langer Lab.

Pursue use-inspired research. Companies could direct their research efforts toward concrete problems whose solutions may hold enormous long-term payoffs in terms of the impact on humanity and the ROI. (Bob Langer estimates that venture capitalists have reaped at least a 50% internal rate of return on their investments in the companies he has helped launch.) Those efforts should be a good fit with the company's deep competencies.

Nurture deep scientific and engineering expertise in a handful of areas. This could bring customers flocking for solutions to their most pressing problems.

Manage intellectual property much more aggressively. Companies could benefit from seeking extremely broad, strong patents. And they could license discoveries they don't want to pursue themselves, both to generate income and to ensure that someone pursues them.

Treat the central research organization as a separate entity, liberated from the incremental demands of established business units. In addition, companies could improve their research efforts if they constrained research projects by time, not by creativity.

Staff labs with great—not merely good—scientists and engineers, with an emphasis on making a difference rather than on job stability. Although a

---

Build a Bridge over the Valley of Death

Choosing the right projects to pursue is just the first step, of course; the path to realization can be long and treacherous. Langer has a formula for getting discoveries through the valley of death separating early-stage research and commercial development.

Focus mostly on "platform technologies"—those with multiple applications

Many corporate and academic labs look to solve specific problems without necessarily thinking beyond them. Langer Lab takes a broader view. In addition to creating a wider market, this strategy number of companies, including Corning, Genentech, Google, IBM, and Novartis, have postdoc positions and sabbatical programs for professors, the vast majority of researchers even at those firms are long-term employees. Companies could instead give highly talented people two- to five-year contracts, and perhaps a piece of the action if their work succeeds. They should insist on team players with the communication skills, patience, and curiosity to excel in a multidisciplinary context. This approach would give them more flexibility in attracting the range of talent they might need to tackle complex problems.

Establish consistency over time in the funding of, organizational approach to, and independence of advanced research units. This is no easy task; at GE, for example, R&D funding has yo-yoed from one CEO to the next. Success may require a board with a deep understanding of the R&D function and the willingness to push back against an emphasis on quarterly profits.

Ensure robust leadership. This means finding and supporting research directors who are highly respected in their fields and who explicitly see their role as liberating and nurturing the talent around them. Such leaders will have strong networks that can be tapped for recruitment and collaborations; a vision of how the company's expertise can be applied to create major new businesses that are in keeping with corporate strategy; the ability to communicate that vision to secure internal funding and external support; and the goal of making the research organization's value blatantly apparent— ensuring that the unit is seen as the engine of renewal.

allows companies to pursue unanticipated applications, says Terry McGuire, a founding partner of Polaris. For example, Momenta, a company launched in 2001 to exploit new methods for understanding and manipulating the structures of sugar molecules, initially set out to sequence heparins in order to treat diseases such as cancer and acute coronary syndrome. However, it realized early on that it could also use the emerging technology to determine the complex structures in Lovenox, an existing multibillion-dollar drug. That work resulted in a biogeneric product for preventing and treating deep vein thrombosis, which generated more than $1 billion in sales during its first year.

Although the lab's researchers often have a use in mind, sometimes they envision a variety of applications. For example, Langer got the idea for an implantable microchip that could release drugs for years and could be controlled outside the body while watching a television show on semiconductors; he imagined that chips could not only be used to deliver drugs but also put into TVs to release scents that would enhance the viewing experience.

Obtain a broad patent

MIT has been a pioneer in patenting and licensing academic discoveries. But Langer has been exceptional in his pursuit of especially strong patents. His goal is to limit, sometimes even block, others from claiming rights to the territory so that companies will be willing to expend the money needed to commercialize a discovery—an investment that must typically cover expensive clinical trials and that greatly exceeds the cost of the research. (Some of Langer's secrets: Use "great lawyers" and have them challenge one another's recommendations; eliminate unnecessary words that could restrict a claim; and clearly describe all the terms and supporting experimental tests to prevent ambiguity if the patent is litigated.)

Publish a seminal article in a prestigious journal

Appearing in a journal such as *Nature* or *Science* validates—and advertises—the soundness and importance of the discovery not just to other academics but also to potential business investors.

Prove the concept in animal studies, and don't push the discovery out of the lab too quickly

The reason is twofold: to boost the odds that the discovery will work and to minimize the chances that commercialization efforts will flounder—a common occurrence in universities and even the corporate world.

One recent example of a project that benefited from a measured timetable involved the use of ultrasound to rapidly deliver a broad class of therapeutics, including small molecules, macromolecule biologics, and nucleic acids, directly to the gastrointestinal tract (they previously had to be injected). Despite promising initial results and the eagerness of one of the lab's scientists to start a company to commercialize the discovery, Langer resisted taking that step just yet. He wanted to keep the lab team intact and to continue to work on the technology—for instance, demonstrating its safety through "chronic treatment" studies in large animals (giving them the treatment, say, daily for a month) and developing new formulations that could further enhance the delivery of the drugs.

This extra research, unfettered by commercial timetables, paid off. Over the next 18 months or so, the lab demonstrated that the technology could deliver a whole new class of drugs (unencapsulated nucleic acids), broadening its potential applications. The team also published more articles on the research in peer-reviewed journals, providing proof that the original data was reliable and replicable. Only then did Langer agree to help raise funds for a new company, Suono Bio, to take over development.

Reward the researchers

MIT awards inventors one-third of royalty income after expenses and fees. (The rest goes to the researchers' departments or centers, MIT's technology-licensing office, and the university's general fund.) In recent decades a growing number of universities have instituted similar policies, but the approach is still highly unusual in the corporate world.

Involve the researchers in commercial development

Over the years many members of the lab have left for positions at companies that took on their projects, where their passion for getting the technology to market has proved as important as their expertise. "One of the reasons a lot of the companies have done well is that the champions have been our students who've gone to them," Langer says. "They really believed in what they did in the lab and wanted to make it a reality." Other researchers have advised companies while remaining at the lab or after moving on to other universities. Langer himself serves on the boards of 10 Boston-area start-ups that have emerged from his work. While a growing number of universities have relaxed restrictions on professors' involving themselves in commercial ventures and have even encouraged commercialization by launching incubators and accelerators, there are still mixed feelings about such activities at many places that lack MIT's established entrepreneurial culture. And in the corporate world, it's highly unusual for scientists to become deeply involved in commercialization.

Make licenses contingent on using the technology
If a firm doesn't make use of technology it has licensed from the lab, it can be made to relinquish the license. And consider how the wafer for treating brain tumors came to market: A company uninterested in the treatment happened to buy the firm that had licensed the technology. MIT got it to agree to launch a start-up to develop the wafer in return for a lower licensing fee. Few universities—or companies— manage their patents as aggressively as MIT does. Consequently, many of their potentially useful discoveries aren't exploited.

Forge a Collaborative Multidisciplinary Team

A team working on an oral drug-delivery device that could sit in the stomach gradually releasing medicine for weeks or months came up with a star-shaped design. Then a mechanical engineer with modeling experience joined the effort and began to ask questions. Why had the team chosen a star? Why not other shapes? The team evaluated several possibilities, including hexagons and a variety of stars, and found that a six-pointed star performed best in terms of its ability to fit inside a capsule and stay in the stomach. The new team member also raised considerations about the stiffness of the arms and center, the strength of the elastomer at the interface, and the size of the unfolded device. This turned the conversation to materials that might enable the device to last longer.

"That's what happens when you bring together folks with different backgrounds," says Giovanni Traverso, a Harvard gastroenterologist, biomedical engineer, and MIT research affiliate who heads the team. "It leads to new insights and new ways of thinking about the problem." The teams at Langer Lab include chemical, mechanical, and electrical engineers; molecular biologists; medical clinicians;

veterinarians; materials scientists; physicists; and pharmaceutical chemists. Members from different disciplines sit side by side in the labs and offices that honeycomb the sixth floor of the Koch Institute.

Multidisciplinary labs are sprouting up as academia recognizes their value in tackling challenges ranging from cancer to global warming. (One of the hallmarks of the Stand Up to Cancer campaign is its funding of such teams.) But the revolution is still in early days. The 2016 MIT report "Convergence: The Future of Health," coauthored by Susan Hockfield, highlights the importance of bringing together engineering, physical, computational, mathematical, and biomedical sciences "to help solve many of the world's grand challenges." It calls for ambitious reforms in education, industry, and government, including the creation of a "culture of convergence" in academia and industry and changes to government research-funding practices.

Langer's reputation, the challenges his lab takes on, and the career opportunities afforded, including the chance to participate in start-ups, attract lots of applicants. The lab has 119 researchers from all over the world, plus 30 to 40 undergraduates each semester. It receives 4,000 to 5,000 applications for the 10 to 20 postdoc positions that open up each year and conducts global searches when specialized skills are needed for particular projects.

It's a given that applicants must have outstanding academic credentials and be highly motivated. Beyond that, the leadership team of Langer, Traverso, and Ana Jaklenec, a biomedical engineer and MIT staff scientist, looks for people who "are nice, get along well with others, and are good communicators"—vital qualities given that the lab's researchers must constantly explain their fields to coworkers and find ways to conduct experiments that work for everyone. Differences in technical languages, work practices, values, and even ways of defining problems constitute one of the most formidable challenges of a multidisciplinary lab, says Hockfield, a champion of convergence during her eight years at MIT's helm.

Jaklenec showed me a whiteboard filled with equations. It was from a meeting of two postdocs—a biologist and a biomedical engineer who were collaborating on a single-injection polio vaccine that could stay in the body and be released in pulses over time. The biologist was

An Unusual Road to High-Impact Research

IN THE EARLY 1970S, AS BOB LANGER was completing a PhD in chemical engineering at MIT, the United States was rocked by the OPEC embargo and the resulting oil crisis—making him a hot commodity in the eyes of oil and chemical companies (he received 20 job offers in the field). An interview at an Exxon operation in Baton Rouge prompted a seminal insight. "One of the engineers said to me, 'If you could just increase the yield of this one chemical by point-one percent, that would be wonderful—that's worth billions of dollars,'" Langer recalls. "I remember flying back to Boston that night thinking, 'Do I really want to spend my life doing this?'"

He applied to colleges for jobs developing chemistry curricula. When none replied—"probably because as a chemical engineer, I wasn't in the right box"—he wrote to hospitals, "because I wanted to help people." Again he received no offers.

Then a colleague suggested that he contact Judah Folkman, a surgeon at Boston Children's Hospital who had a reputation for hiring unusual people. Folkman had a controversial idea: that cancerous tumors emit chemical signals that stimulate angiogenesis, or the formation of new blood vessels. If the signals could be blocked, Folkman theorized, tumors' growth could be halted. He hired Langer to isolate the first angiogenesis inhibitors. This involved iden-

exploring the mechanism that degrades the strain of virus used in the vaccine, while the biomedical engineer was working on thermostabilization. The two encountered a problem: Their data sets didn't make sense together. It turned out that they had run their experiments with different concentrations of the vaccine: The engineer's were those used clinically, while the biologist's were those called for by the analytical methods of her field. The researchers had to align their experiments so that they could compare results. Such issues are not uncommon. "The challenge is to get people to talk the same language and also recognize that for certain things, there's no single expert," Traverso says.

Even if there is no obvious need or fit for them, Langer often brings in "superstars" who have unusual credentials. "You take a chance on people," he says. "Gio is a good example." Traverso had earned a PhD in molecular biology under Bert Vogelstein, a renowned cancer biologist at Johns Hopkins; his doctoral research involved tifying candidates from cartilage, which has no blood supply (Langer got cow bones from a slaughterhouse) and inventing polymer systems that could deliver large molecules over time. Angiogenesis inhibitors ultimately became instrumental in treating a number of cancers, and polymers have become an important way to deliver drugs and vaccines and to help grow new body tissue, including skin, cartilage, and spinal cord.

Langer returned to MIT in 1977 as an assistant professor, initially in the Department of Nutrition and Food Science (because no chemical engineering department at a university would hire him). It gave him tremendous freedom, and he continued working on drug delivery, angiogenesis inhibitors, and tissue engineering, obtaining funding from companies when his ideas proved too radical for government grants. Many senior faculty members of the department didn't believe in his ideas and suggested that he look for a new job. However, by the mid-1980s his discoveries, publications, and start-ups began winning recognition. One of MIT's 13 Institute Professors, Langer is a member of the National Academies of Sciences, Engineering, and Medicine, and a recipient of the National Medal of Technology and Innovation, the National Medal of Science, the Charles Stark Draper Prize, and the Queen Elizabeth Prize for Engineering.

novel molecular tests for the early detection of colon cancer. When he contacted Langer, he was finishing an internal medicine residency at Boston's Brigham and Women's Hospital and trying to figure out what to do with a gastroenterology fellowship he had landed at Massachusetts General Hospital. He told Langer that although he was interested in developing systems for delivering drugs in the GI tract, he was not an engineer. Langer hired him anyway.

The bet paid off. Traverso demonstrated the concept of several different approaches to delivering drugs through devices in the GI tract. The Gates Foundation saw that the work might solve problems it wanted to address in poor countries and provided significant funding. Grants also came in from Novo Nordisk (to develop microneedles for internal injections), the Charles Stark Draper Lab (for new ingestible systems), and Hoffmann-La Roche (for the delivery of a new class of drugs).

Embrace Turnover

Like all academic labs, Langer's sees a constant flow of people join-ing or leaving. Doctoral students typically stay four or five years, postdocs two or three, and undergraduates participate for as little as a semester and as much as four years. Newcomers are perpetually being trained, and people may leave at the peak of their productiv-ity. But Langer and many colleagues think the turnover has positives that vastly outweigh these downsides. Problems are viewed with fresh eyes—he calls it "constant stimulation." The turnover is fairly predictable and tied to the length of projects; even huge grants are structured so that the lab can gradually scale up. The finite tenure of most of the researchers, combined with the limited duration of grants (typically three to five years, with renewals dependent on meeting goals), imposes pressure to get results.

"A lot of cynicism has been thrown on the academic research lab model. We are told it is inefficient," Hockfield says. "But it's brilliant. To bring together people from different generations and levels of experience—it's fantastic. The faculty member has a wealth of expe-rience and understanding and knows the literature and the history of the field. Students and postdocs have a lot of energy and ambi-tion and crazy ideas. The faculty member helps get those crazy ideas channeled. Undergraduates, wonderfully, often don't know that something's impossible. They don't know enough not to ask unso-phisticated questions. There are very few things that make you step back and wonder about your foundational assumptions more than a really smart undergraduate asking, 'Whoa, how does that work?'"

A highly motivated superstar team with limited tenure; an accomplished scientist leader; time-limited projects; intense pres-sure to get results—it all sounds like the DARPA formula, proof that the model has application far beyond academic settings.

Lead Without Micromanaging

One rainy day at their home on Cape Cod, Langer and his wife, Laura, talked about how his management of the lab differs from the norm. "In my discussions with a range of graduate students at other places, they often describe their research advisers as control freaks—which is understandable, because their lab is their baby," said Laura, who has a PhD in neuroscience from MIT. "They may want to manage every part of the research. It's very hard for them to let their students explore and make mistakes. But not giving people the room to figure things out themselves can stifle them or train them to not take potentially innovative risks."

Langer nodded in agreement. Under his leadership, everyone is involved in offering ideas for projects and choosing which ones to pursue. "It's a team effort," he said. "It's empowering people; it's letting everybody feel they are valued and that it's OK to suggest things." This stands in contrast to most academic and corporate labs, where the director selects the projects.

Current and former lab members told me that Langer exposes people to possibilities and lets them decide what to work on. Gordana Vunjak-Novakovic, a professor of biomedical engineering and medical sciences at Columbia who worked at the lab in the 1980s and 1990s, says she took that lesson to heart and runs her 40-person lab the same way: "I never tell people what to do but, rather, help them see the possibilities, let them really get excited about one of them, and let them work on their own ideas." Many if not most of Langer's postdocs and research scientists and at least some of the doctoral students are working on several projects. (For a fuller picture of life in Langer Lab, see the profile of two postdocs in the online version of this article, at HBR.org.)

Langer treats Jaklenec and Traverso as coprincipal investigators—another departure from the norm. Power is distributed throughout the lab, accumulated on the basis of people's ideas and initiative and the funding that their research attracts. Langer gives researchers—especially graduate students—lots of guidance in the beginning, to make sure that they get off to a good start and that projects are optimally structured. He also helps decide which options are considered. For example, at the outset of the project to develop the drug-delivery device that would stay in the stomach for a long period, he and Traverso decided to explore two possibilities: one that would

Real-World Results

SINCE 1987 BOB LANGER and his researchers have helped found 40 companies, often in collaboration with scientists in other labs at MIT and at other institutions. To date all but one have made it. A sampling is below.

Company: Enzytech (acquired by Alkermes)
Year launched: 1987
Products/technology: Microspheres for delivering drugs
Existing or potential applications: Schizophrenia, narcotic addiction, type 2 diabetes
Market capitalization: $7.2 billion (Alkermes)

Company: Moderna
Year launched: 2011
Products/technology: Messenger-RNA-based drugs
Existing or potential applications: Cancer, heart disease, vaccines, infectious diseases, pulmonary disease
Market capitalization: $5 billion

Company: Momenta
Year launched: 2001
Products/technology: Sequencing complex sugar-based therapeutics
Existing or potential applications: Multiple sclerosis and other autoimmune diseases, cardiovascular diseases, cancer
Market capitalization: $840 million

Company: Advanced Inhalation Research (acquired by Acorda)
Year launched: 1997
Products/technology: Drug-delivering aerosols that rely on large particles, which resist clumping
Existing or potential applications: Diabetes, asthma, Parkinson's disease
Market capitalization: $525 million

Company: Selecta
Year launched: 2007
Products/technology: Targeted nanoparticle-based immunotherapies and vaccines
Existing or potential applications: Gout, genetic disorders, allergies, autoimmune diseases, HPV-associated cancers, nicotine addiction, malaria
Market capitalization: $228 million

Sources: Robert Langer, Polaris Partners, public information.
Note: Market capitalizations are as of mid-September 2016 or acquisition date. The value of private companies is based on VC financing.

float in the stomach and one that would adhere to the stomach wall. After conducting a feasibility study, they chose to pursue the floating option and figured out what major issues would need to be solved—and then Langer largely bowed out. "After that, I don't tell people what to do," he says. "From grade school to high school and college and even to a certain extent graduate school, you're judged by how well you answer somebody else's questions. That gives you a grade on a test. But if you think about the way you're judged in life, I don't think it is by how good your answers are; it's by how good your questions are. I want to help people make that transition from giving good answers to asking good questions."

Gary Pisano sees this philosophy as key to the lab's success. "The tendency would be to say, 'I'm going to tell you what to do so that you can do better and the lab will do better,'" he explains. "But if you do that, you create a different place—people are going to say, 'OK, Bob, you tell me what to do.' He doesn't want that kind of lab. His lab is one where people solve their own problems, and that's why they wind up being great professors and scientists in the business world."

At the same time, Langer makes sure that researchers know they can count on him and on the people in his network if they run into trouble—an approach that Aimee L. Hamilton, an assistant professor of management at the University of Denver who has studied Langer Lab, calls "guided autonomy." His responsiveness is legendary. His iPad seems glued to him, and he uses it to answer e-mails within minutes. Cato T. Laurencin, a University Professor at the University of Connecticut who earned his PhD under Langer in the 1980s, recalls that a student of his once dug up Langer's cell phone number and called him with a question about a paper Langer had written. "He called her back from Finland 10 minutes later."

Langer also goes out of his way to help people leaving his lab get good jobs, and he stays in touch with hundreds of alumni, providing assistance if needed. (In his farewell meeting with James Dahlman, he offered to go over Dahlman's grant applications.) He is deeply connected to those in his network. For instance, he refers to many of the venture capitalists who have financed his start-ups—a group including Terry McGuire, of Polaris; Noubar Afeyan, of Flagship;

and Mark Levin, of Third Rock—as friends, and means it. (Langer, McGuire, and their two daughters vacationed together last year in Bordeaux, and Langer's daughter was in the wedding of McGuire's.)

The investment in his network pays valuable dividends in the form of productive research collaborations, referrals of extraordinary students to his lab, and manpower for the start-ups. Langer not only paves the way for lab members to launch start-ups but also taps his network if a need at one emerges down the road. "Bob often has a great idea of somebody who would be a great fit," says Amy Schulman, the CEO or executive chair of three companies that grew out of Langer Lab. "And people often reach out to Bob when they're thinking of changing jobs, because he is incredibly discreet and knows a lot of opportunities. So it goes both ways."

When people who have worked with Bob Langer talk about him, one hears a common refrain: He is an integral part of his research-to-product model and a brilliant individual who can't be replicated. But this doesn't mean that his model, including his "Mr. Nice Guy" leadership style, can't be replicated. What if corporations structured their labs like his? What if they nurtured deep expertise in a handful of areas so that customers would come to them with their most pressing problems? What if they enticed superstar researchers by offering opportunities to work on issues that could change the world?

"Maybe companies could set up a research operation where the best of the best are flowing through, trying to do something audacious in a few years rather than spending 30 years there worrying about their next promotion," Gary Pisano says. His Harvard colleague Willy Shih adds that such an approach would not only allow companies to tackle more-ambitious projects but also help them kill mediocre or poor projects faster. "The flow of people through the lab would have the natural consequence of sunsetting ideas that don't stand the test of a fresh look," he points out.

Bob Langer says, "I want to address problems that can change the world and make it a better place. That's the thread throughout the science I've done my whole life. The companies I've helped found seem like a natural extension. I wanted to see what I did get out to the world; that made a difference to me." By drawing on the Langer Lab values and model, companies could make the world a better place and make lots of money in the process.

Further Reading

FOR MORE ON REVITALIZING your research operations, see these articles on HBR.org.

- **"Getting Your Stars to Collaborate,"** Heidi K. Gardner (January–February 2017)

- **"You Need an Innovation Strategy,"** Gary P. Pisano (June 2015)

- **"'Special Forces' Innovation: How DARPA Attacks Problems,"** Regina E. Dugan and Kaigham J. Gabriel (October 2013)

- **"Rebuilding the R&D Engine in Big Pharma,"** Jean-Pierre Garnier (May 2008)

Originally published in March–April 2017. Reprint R1702L

About the Contributors

RON ADNER is a professor of strategy and entrepreneurship at Dartmouth College's Tuck School of Business, where he holds the David T. McLaughlin D'54, T'55 endowed chair.

SCOTT BERINATO is a senior editor at HBR and the author of *Good Charts: The HBR Guide to Making Smarter, More Persuasive Data Visualizations* (Harvard Business Review Press, 2016), from which this article is adapted.

TOM BLASER is a managing director at The Greatest Good Group (TGG Group).

PETER CAPPELLI is a professor of management at the Wharton School and the author of several books, including *Will College Pay Off? A Guide to the Most Important Financial Decision You'll Ever Make* (PublicAffairs, 2015).

FRANK DOBBIN is a professor of sociology at Harvard University.

LINNEA GANDHI is a managing director at TGG Group.

FRANCESCA GINO is a professor at Harvard Business School, a faculty affiliate of the Behavioral Insights Group at Harvard Kennedy School, and the author of *Sidetracked: Why Our Decisions Get Derailed, and How We Can Stick to the Plan* (Harvard Business Review Press, 2013). She cochairs an HBS executive education program on applying behavioral economics to organizational problems.

MARCO IANSITI is the David Sarnoff Professor of Business Administration at Harvard Business School.

DANIEL KAHNEMAN is the Eugene Higgins Professor of Psychology Emeritus at Princeton University. He was awarded the Nobel Prize in Economic Sciences in 2002 for his work (with Amos Tversky) on cognitive biases.

ALEXANDRA KALEV is an associate professor of sociology at Tel Aviv University.

ROBERT S. KAPLAN is a senior fellow and the Marvin Bower Professor of Leadership Development, Emeritus, at Harvard Business School. He is the coauthor (with Michael E. Porter) of "How to Solve the Cost Crisis in Health Care" (HBR, September 2011).

RAHUL KAPOOR is an associate professor of management at the Wharton School.

A.G. LAFLEY, the recently retired CEO of Procter & Gamble, serves on the board of Snap Inc. He is the coauthor (with Roger L. Martin) of *Playing to Win: How Strategy Really Works* (Harvard Business Review Press, 2013).

KARIM R. LAKHANI is a professor of business administration at Harvard Business School and the principal investigator of the Crowd Innovation Laboratory at the Harvard Institute for Quantitative Social Science.

ROGER L. MARTIN is a former dean of the Rotman School of Management at the University of Toronto. He is the coauthor (with A.G. Lafley) of *Playing to Win: How Strategy Really Works* (Harvard Business Review Press, 2013).

RITA GUNTHER MCGRATH, a professor of management at Columbia Business School, is a globally recognized expert on strategy, innovation, and growth with an emphasis on corporate entrepreneurship.

MICHAEL E. PORTER is a University Professor at Harvard, based at Harvard Business School in Boston. He is the coauthor (with Robert S. Kaplan) of "How to Solve the Cost Crisis in Health Care" (HBR, September 2011).

STEVEN PROKESCH is a senior editor at *Harvard Business Review*.

ANDREW M. ROSENFIELD is the CEO and managing partner of TGG Group.

ANNA TAVIS is the academic director of Columbia's program in human capital management and the Perspectives editor at *People + Strategy,* a journal for HR executives.

JOAN C. WILLIAMS is Distinguished Professor of Law and Founding Director of the Center of WorkLife Law at the University of California, Hastings College of the Law. Her newest book is *White Working Class: Overcoming Class Cluelessness in America* (Harvard Business Review Press, 2017).

Index

The most important management ideas all in one place.

We hope you enjoyed this book from *Harvard Business Review*. Now you can get even more with HBR's 10 Must Reads Boxed Set. From books on leadership and strategy to managing yourself and others, this 6-book collection delivers articles on the most essential business topics to help you succeed.

HBR's 10 Must Reads Series

The definitive collection of ideas and best practices on our most sought-after topics from the best minds in business.

- Change Management
- Collaboration
- Communication
- Emotional Intelligence
- Innovation
- Leadership
- Making Smart Decisions

- Managing Across Cultures
- Managing People
- Managing Yourself
- Strategic Marketing
- Strategy
- Teams
- The Essentials

hbr.org/mustreads

Buy for your team, clients, or event.
Visit hbr.org/bulksales for quantity discount rates.